D1642968

ACOL-ITE'S QUIZ

C O L L I N S
WINNING BRIDGE
ACOL-ITE'S
QUIZ
RHODA LEDERER

CollinsWillow
An Imprint of HarperCollins*Publishers*

First published in 1962 by George Allen & Unwin Ltd
Second edition 1968
Reprinted seven times
Third edition published in 1979 by Unwin® Paperbacks
Fourth edition 1981
Reprinted 1982, 1984 (twice)
Fifth edition 1984
Reprinted 1985, 1986, 1987, 1988, 1989, 1990

Revised edition published in 1993 by
Collins Willow
an imprint of HarperCollins*Publishers*, London

**A CIP catalogue record for this book
is available from the British Library**

ISBN 0 00 218444 3

Set in Palatino
Printed and bound in Great Britain
by Cox & Wyman Ltd

Contents

Preface

There are six sections in this book, each of which opens with a summary of the rules covering the particular aspect of bidding being considered. These summaries are not intended as a complete explanation of the Acol System which should, of course, be learned from the main text-book, *All About Acol* or in a more elementary form from *The ABC of Contract Bridge*. They will, however, give the reader the main points with which he or she should be familiar, either as a learner, prospective Acol player, or an Acol player who wants to make sure the bidding is on the right lines.

After each summary comes a series of exercises, each answer being accompanied by an analysis of why a particular bid should be chosen. For instance, a bid may be recommended because it is the only one to express the strength, weakness, or 'shape' of the hand, or the choice of possible alternatives may be conditioned by the need to allow for a sensible rebid on the next round of the auction. You will find that all the most common situations, as well as many far less common and even rare ones, have been covered. Amongst the former are examples of the use of 'directional asking bids' and 'fourth suit forcing', mysteries still to many who would regard themselves as competent bidders. If you want to work through these exercises with a friend or 'opponent' it may add to the interest of your study – take it in turns to answer and keep a record of your hits and misses.

Next in each section comes a further series headed 'Competition Quiz'. These questions can, of course, be worked on your own, or they can be used with advantage by bridge teachers for their students, though they are intended primarily as an amusing and instructive game for two people.

Before we come to the method of using the Competition Quizzes as a game, there are one or two points to consider. First, remember that, in the ranks of the experts and tournament players, many variations, complications, and partnership 'gadgets', not to mention different interpretations of various bidding sequences, exist. The embryo or club player need not concern himself with these. The examples throughout this book echo the basic system as set out in *All About Acol* and, if you stick to these, you should find yourself able to play comfortably in any company with the minimum difficulty and maximum efficiency.

Second, a complete section has been devoted to the development of sequences starting with a no-trump bid, because their inclusion in the other sections would have made these unwieldy. Responses and rebids following a no-trump opening have quite different rules which can be much more clearly covered on their own.

Lastly, the importance of reading the question carefully can't be too highly stressed. If details such as whether or not you are vulnerable, whether or not you are the dealer, or whether another player has opened the bidding or intervened are given, it is because they are relevant to the answer. Don't make mistakes simply through failure to notice these important details.

Competition quiz

As a game between two people, each in turn should answer a complete set of questions as instructed at the head of that quiz. Points are awarded, both for finding the correct bid and for giving the correct reason for this choice, and the game, of course, consists of trying to gain more points on your set of questions than your opponent.

If you fail to give the correct bid you can't thereafter score points for giving the correct reason! But if your bid is right you can earn further points by knowing why you made it. It is more than possible to make the right bid for the wrong reason, or even to make what is no more than a lucky guess and hit the jackpot. A good Acol player must, however, know why he is making any particular bid – a lucky guess won't ensure the right action at the bridge table or in a slightly different set of circumstances.

Your wording for your reasons will inevitably differ from that in the quiz answers, but it should not be difficult to judge whether it is basically correct. For example, if the required rebid is 2NT and the printed reason is that a hand of 16+ to 18 points justifies this bid, you clearly know what you are about if you have said that it is too strong for a rebid of 1NT and not strong enough for 3NT. In other words, you know why you are bidding 2NT, and should score your extra points.

In some instances you will find that you are asked for two bids and, therefore, two reasons, on one quiz hand, with half the available points awarded for each bid and reason. These are divided equally between the **A** and **B** sets of questions to make fair competition.

If you prefer to go through these competition quizzes without an opponent, you should still keep a record of the points you have gained. You could score a maximum of 180 points on each of the **A** and **B** sets, and double that, of course, if you have done both sets on your own. Whether or not you have won or lost to an opponent, have fun grading your ability as an Acol bidder from the table below.

Maximum points available on **A** and **B** questions in each section separately:

Bidding ... 72 points, Reasons ... 108 points, Total ... 180 points.

Score:

170–180 points	Only two mistakes in 36 problems – your partners are lucky to play with you – only don't let it go to your head.
140–169 points	Still reasonably good for a student, but it allows for you to make up to six mistakes in thirty-six bids, too many to be regarded as really efficient.

90–139 points   Allowing for lucky guesses, a fair score for a
                 learner, but the lower end of the range means
                 a wrong bid as often as a right one – you're
                 not yet a sound Acol bidder.

Below 90 points There is still much work to be done but don't
                 give up!

Section 1

Opening Bids

The basic rules

The first requirement of a dealer's or second-in-hand one-level opening bid is that it should contain a sensible rebid. The reason for this is that partner's change-of-suit response is a one-round force. As third or fourth hand, priority may be given to consideration of whether or not it is expedient to open, either to obstruct or to direct partner's lead, as once partner has passed originally, a change-of-suit response from him is no longer forcing.

An opening bid should aim at expressing as much of the hand as possible – clarification will come at the rebid, if any. But the strongest bid for which the hand qualifies should always be chosen. Thus a one-level bid denies the ability to open at the two-level, and a strong two opening denies the ability to open 2♣. Even a 2♣ opening denies a hand suitable for an immediate 4NT or five of a major.

1 *Suit opening bids at the one-level:*

9–11 points	Tactical light opening bids with a six-card suit or two five-card suits as long as these provide a safe rebid.
12 or more points	Five-card suit, a five and a four-card suit, or two four-card suits, as long as these provide a sensible rebid.

Up to 20 points	Except if fitted for a no-trump opening, and if not suitable for a strong two or 2♣ bid, should be opened at the one-level and excess strength by a strong rebid.
20 or more points	Almost always qualify for better than a one-bid. Hands of 4–4–4–1 pattern with no playing strength by way of suit length are possible exceptions.
4–4–4–1 'shape'	Because of lack of trump length, minimum count should be 13 points. Open one of the suit below the singleton except when the singleton is clubs, when open 1♡. If only two of the three suits are 'biddable', treat as a two-suiter (see below).
Two four-card suits	Unless suitable for a no-trump opening bid, with adjacent suits bid higher-ranking first, except with ♣ and ♠, when bid ♣ first. With ♠ and ◇ + ♡ support, ♠ first; with ♠ and ◇ + ♣ support, bid ◇ first; with ♡ and ♣ + ◇ support, ♡ first; with ♡ and ♣ + ♠ support, ♣ first.
1♣ and 1◇	'Prepared' minor suit openings are admissible when the hand otherwise contains no sensible rebid. The minor so bid should contain at least three cards to one of the three top honours. If both qualify, bid 1♣.

2 *No-trump opening bids:*

1NT weak (12–14 points)	This is the prescribed strength for a non-vulnerable opening 1NT. Preferably evenly-balanced hand with a guard in all suits. A five-card suit is not prohibited.
1NT strong (15–17 points)	The prescribed strength when vulnerable, of the same type as the above, except with extra honour count. Highly unlikely to contain a five-card major as this could be bid at the one-level.

Note: The above is known as 'variable no-trump', but the opening strength is optional and based on partnership agreement. 'Weak throughout', 'strong throughout', or other variations are permitted as long as these are announced to the opponents and there is no more than a 3–point spread (12–14, 13–15, etc).

2NT (20–22 points)	The same values at any score. Should include a stop in all suits. A balanced hand is recommended though a five-card suit, particularly a minor, is not prohibited.
23–24 points	These values are shown by an opening bid of 2♣ followed by a rebid of 2NT.
25 or more points	Again, if in a no-trump type hand, these values are shown by an opening bid of 2♣, and this is followed by a rebid of 3NT.
3NT	A tactical opening bid based on a long and solid minor suit. Need not concern the learner at this stage.
4NT	Conventional, showing interest *only* in partner's ace-holding, if any. The conventional responses are: with no ace, 5♣; with ◇A, ♡A, ♠A, cue-bid five of the ace-suit; with ♣A, bid 6♣, and with two aces bid 5NT.

3 *Strong two opening bids:*

2◇, 2♡, 2♠	a Single-suited hands containing not less than eight playing tricks at the suit named. b Powerful two-suiters likely to develop eight tricks if the best fit is found. c Powerful hands lacking the nine playing tricks which are needed for a 2♣ opening, but on which there is a danger that the balance of the points may be so divided that a one-level opening may be passed out when little support is needed for a successful game contract. Strong two openings are forcing for one round, the negative response being 2NT.

The emphasis is on playing tricks – do NOT count points for this bid.

4 2♣ opening bids:

23–24 points	Powerful no-trump type hands, shown by a rebid of 2NT. The only 2♣ opening which may be passed below game-level.
25+ points	Even more powerful no-trump type hands, 2♣ followed by 3NT rebid.
2♣ with a suit rebid	A powerful game-going hand with a minimum of nine playing tricks and playing strength by way of a good trump suit or suits. The suit rebid makes the sequence forcing to game.

There are two negative responses available, first 2◇, and then 2NT if no more constructive bid can next be found.

5 Pre-emptive opening bids:

3-level or more	Hands based on one very long suit, worthless in defence or, generally, four cards in any unbid major.
3NT	See under 2 on page 15.
4-level in majors	Long strong major suit and not more than two defensive tricks. Partner is not expected to respond if he has already passed or, if not yet having had a chance to bid, to make a slam try on less than two aces.
5-level in minors	Both four and five-level opening bids in the minors are purely pre-emptive, based on very long suits and with no foreseeable defence against the majors.

6 Conventional high-level suit openings:

5-level in ♡ or ♠	Requests responder to bid the small slam with *either* the ace *or* the king of the suit opened, even if the honour card is a singleton, and to bid the grand

slam if holding both the ace and king. *No* other honour holdings will be of any interest to opener.

6-level in ♡ or ♠	Can be used when, for a grand slam, opener is missing only the ace *or* king of his trump suit. Responder should raise to the grand slam if holding either, even if singleton.
6-level in ♣ or ◇	Can be used as above in the minors, but *not* at the 5-level, as these minor suit openings are used pre-emptively and not conventionally.

Exercises

1   ♠ A Q J 9 6 2   As dealer at any score, what action
    ♡ 9 5   would you take?
    ◇ 8
    ♣ K 10 9 5

Answer: It is always important to consider whether an opening bid, particularly on a hand which is light in honour strength, is likely to do more harm than good to your side. But an early attack almost always pays dividends provided the hand contains a sensible rebid. As a change-of-suit response from partner is a one-round force, this is a very necessary consideration.

A six-card suit which can be bid and rebid as a sign-off constitutes an excellent reason for opening. Not only will you have gone into the attack early, but you will have indicated a line of defence to partner if, later, you become a defender.

(Bid: 1♠)

2   ♠ K 10 8 6 5   As dealer with the score Game All,
    ♡ A K Q J 9   what action would you take on this
    ◇ 9 3   hand?
    ♣ 4

Answer: With 13 points and two five-card majors you would always open the bidding, whatever your position at the table and whatever the score.

Here your choice is simple – with two equal and adjacent suits the rule is to open one of the higher-ranking first, which gives you a safe rebid in the other. It doesn't matter that the hearts are so much stronger – they will come in useful anyway. The important point is to give yourself the best chance to tell your partner that you have a biddable spade suit and, if the auction comes round to you again, a biddable heart suit too. Unless he has strong ideas of his own, he will then be in a position to let you play in the one which fits his hand best.

(Bid: 1♠)

3   ♠ A Q 10 7   As dealer, whatever the score,
    ♡ K J 8   what opening bid would you make
    ◊ 3 2   on this hand?
    ♣ A Q 10 7

Answer: The rules for your choice between two four-card suits are the same as for five-card suits. With equal and adjacent suits bid the higher-ranking first. With non-adjacent suits other considerations may come into it, as we shall see later.

Meanwhile here's another rule – with equal-lengthed *black* suits in a hand qualifying for no better than a one-bid, *bid the clubs first*. This has two advantages: firstly, having started with 1♣ you have a simple rebid of 1♠ if partner responds in a red suit; and, secondly, as the auction develops, he will be able to tell that you have at least as many clubs as spades, if not more. As you should always try to bid a longer suit before a shorter, and as a suit is not *re*biddable if it is of less than five-card length, if you open 1♣ and subsequently bid and rebid spades, showing that the second suit is rebiddable, or of at least five-cards, then your hand must contain at least ten black cards. Here you could not rebid either black suit.

(Bid: 1♣)

4   ♠ K 10 8 6 5   This is the same hand as 2 except
    ♡ 9 3   that the red suits have changed
    ◊ A K Q J 9   places. What dealer's opening bid,
    ♣ 4   if any, would you make?

Answer: This time your suits are not adjacent, and you must give careful thought to the future of the auction. If you open 1 ◊ and responder bids 1♡, all is well as you rebid 1♠, which is neither forcing nor unduly encouraging. But if responder bids 2♣ over 1◊, you would have to show your spades at the two-level, which is reserved for much stronger hands. This would mean falling back on a rebid of 2◊, for ever concealing your five-card major.

If, however, you open 1♠, you can safely rebid 2◊ over a response of 2♣, and if the response to 1♠ is 2♡, you rebid 2♠, at least not having concealed your major suit. Certainly you may have to bid a little untruthfully, but all kinds of things may have happened to the auction before you have to bid a second time.

(Bid: 1♠)

5	♠ A Q 9 5	Would you open on this hand and,
	♡ 6	if so, what would you bid? Would
	◊ K Q 8 2	it make any difference if your
	♣ K J 8 3	diamonds were changed to ◊Q–10–8–2?

Answer: The first rule for 4–4–4–1 hands with three biddable suits is to open one of the suit below the singleton, so you bid 1◊. This is, of course, bearing in mind the need for a sensible rebid, as if partner responds 1♡ you can bid 1♠, and if he responds 2♣ you can raise him, knowing a spade fit has not been missed.

With the ◊K missing your hand would be worth only 12 points, and though there are many 'shapes' on which this would be more than ample, 4–4–4–1 isn't one of them. There is no playing strength by way of a long suit so that if you are forced to ruff hearts early on, the hand may well fall to pieces. 4–4–4–1 hands should contain a minimum of 13 points, and preferably more.

(Bids: 1◊ and No Bid)

6	♠ A Q 9 5	This is the same hand as 5 except
	♡ K J 8 3	that the clubs have become hearts.
	◊ K Q 8 2	What difference, if any, would this
	♣ 6	make to your correct opening bid?

Answer: The choice of opening bid must frequently be based on thought for the future. If you open 1♠, which is now technically 'the suit below the singleton', you will be able to do no better than guess what to bid next if partner responds 2♣. Whichever you choose, you may miss a good fit in the other.

Assuming that partner will normally elect to make a spade response if he can do so, if you open 1♡ you make it easy for him to respond 1♠ and, if he still bids 2♣, you are pretty sure no spade fit has been missed, so can rebid 2♢ quite happily. If he responds 2♢ or raises hearts, you've found the fit anyway.

So the rule set out in hand 5 now has an addition. Open one of the suit below the singleton except when the singleton is in clubs, when open 1♡.

(Bid: 1♡)

7 ♠ 7   What opening bid would you
   ♡ 6 5 4 3   make on this 4–4–4–1 hand?
   ♢ A Q 9 5
   ♣ A K 9 2

Answer: This time only two of the three four-card suits can really be considered 'biddable' in a 13-point hand. In other words, the heart suit is not one you want to suggest as the trump suit unless partner can bid it, when you would, of course, support him.

Treating this hand as a minor two-suiter, therefore, you simply open 1♢, the higher-ranking. If partner responds 1♠ you can rebid 2♣ with a clear conscience, and if instead he responds 1♡, the least you can do is to raise him to 3♡. A direct raise to 4♡ would be stretching things too far, as responder might have a mere 6 points for his one-level response. If he has more, he should be capable of taking the hint!

(Bid: 1♢)

8 ♠ A J 9   At Love All, what opening bid
   ♡ K J 9 8   would you make?
   ♢ K 8 4
   ♣ J 10 8

Answer: This depends on the agreed strength of your no-trump opening, which is one of the optional features of the Acol System. You can agree 'weak throughout', which means 12–14 points at any score, 'strong throughout', which means 15–17 points at any score, or 'variable', which means weak when not vulnerable and strong when vulnerable. You will find that there are also other variations in use, particularly in the tournament world.

In these quizzes we shall work on 'variable', so be sure to learn what this means now. In this way you will learn to handle both 'weak' and 'strong', and can decide which you prefer.

1NT is the perfect opening bid on this hand when using the weak variety. It is evenly-balanced, contains 13½ points (tens count ½ a point in no-trump bidding if working with other honours) and has 'something in everything'.

(Bid: 1NT)

9 ♠ K J 8	At Game All, using a variable no-
♡ K J 9 8	trump, what opening bid would
◊ A 9 8	you make on this hand?
♣ J 6 2	

Answer: Using a weak no-trump this would be the perfect bid on this hand but you are not strong enough for a 15–17 point no-trump opening – it's important not to promise a minimum of 15 points when you have, in fact, only 13. Nor are you strong enough to open 1♡, your four-card suit, as this could well put you into difficulties for a truthful rebid. This is one of the rare occasions when you must fall back on a 'prepared' minor suit opening of 1♣.

(Bid: 1♣)

10 ♠ A J 10 8	At Game All, what opening bid
♡ K J 10 7	would you make on this hand?
◊ A J	
♣ A 7 4	

Answer: Whatever the score you are too strong to open 1NT on this hand, as even a strong no-trump promises *not more* than 17 points. Nor is this the moment for a 'prepared' 1♣, even though the suit qualifies, so think again! *Never* make a prepared bid on a hand with a sensible alternative.

1♠, the higher-ranking of equal and adjacent suits, would be a lesser evil than 1♣, but there is an even better bid available. This is a strong hand admirably suited to play in no-trumps if partner responds in a minor suit, but splendidly equipped for a game in either major if partner has a four-card fit. On the grounds that he will respond in spades if he can, make it easy for him. Open 1♡ and rebid 3NT if he bids 2♣ or 2♢. If he responds 1♠, however, raise to 4♠ (cf. hand 7). In this way you won't miss a heart fit either.

(Bid: 1♡)

11 ♠ Q 8 6 4   As dealer, what opening bid would
    ♡ A Q 9 3   you make on this hand?
    ♢ A Q 9 8 5
    ♣ –

Answer: The rules for opening suit bids are quite clear – the longer suit before the shorter, the higher-ranking before the lower, and the stronger before the weaker. But these, as we have already seen, must give way to the need to consider an honest rebid.

The rule covering this hand is, of course, the first, so you open 1♢, knowing that you can support partner strongly if he responds in either major, and that your diamonds are good enough to *re*bid if he responds in clubs. This should be your guide before you decide, as well you might, to treat this hand as you would do a 4–4–4–1 distribution with a singleton club, on which you would open 1♡. Take some of your diamond honour strength out into your spades, and you would not want to put yourself into the position of having to rebid the diamonds. Only then would you open 1♡ and risk subsequent preference to a suit you don't actually prefer.

(Bid: 1♢)

12 ♠ A J 9 7   As dealer at Game All, what open-
    ♡ K 8 7   ing bid would you make on this
    ♢ A Q 6 2   hand?
    ♣ 5 3

Answer: You must choose, of course, between your two four-card suits, and you can't get yourself off the hook of this decision by bidding 1NT for which you are too weak. Nor, incidentally, would the hand make a good weak no-trump opening containing, as it does, a worthless doubleton and a sensible alternative bid.

In this case you are able to keep to the rule about opening the higher-ranking suit before the lower, that is, you open 1♠. Working out the likely development of the auction, you can see that this leaves you a sensible rebid. If partner responds 2♣ you can safely rebid 2◊, and if he responds either 2◊ or 2♡, you can raise. If you make the mistake of opening 1◊ you have no problem if the response is 1♡, but you have nothing sensible to say if the response is 2♣.

(Bid: 1♠)

13 ♠ A J 9 7   As dealer at Game All, what open-
   ♡ 5 3   ing bid would you make on this
   ◊ A Q 6 2   hand?
   ♣ K 8 7

Answer: This is the same hand as 12, except that the hearts and clubs have changed places, though this makes all the difference.

On 12 you opened 1♠ because you realised that this was the bid best calculated to make your rebid simple. This time, if you open 1♠ and partner bids 2♣ you can happily rebid 2◊, but you are in difficulties if, instead, he bids 2♡. With one more point – say the ♣J – you could bid 2NT but as it is, not only were you under strength for a strong no-trump opening, but you are under strength for a 2NT rebid. Open 1◊, which gives you a sensible rebid of 1♠ to a response of 1♡, or a raise in clubs to a response of 2♣. If partner can't himself produce a further bid, you don't want to be in a high-level contract on a somewhat flat 14 points.

(Bid: 1◊)

14 ♠ 5 3   As dealer at Game All, what open-
   ♡ A J 9 7   ing bid would you make on this
   ◊ K 8 7   hand?
   ♣ A Q 6 2

Answer: Note that here, as well as in hands 12 and 13, you were vulnerable which means that, using a variable no-trump, you had no option but to pick one of your suits for your opening bid. As before, work out the probable development of the auction to help you to decide between your alternatives of 1♣ and 1♡.

If you open 1♣ and the response is 1♠, what are you to bid next? Your only course would be to fall back on 1NT which might well mean missing a far better contract. If, however, you open 1♡, you can rebid 2♣ in reply to partner's 1♠, or raise him if he bids 2◊.

You will see from these examples that, with two four-card suits, and when your count prohibits a 1NT opening, your choice may be conditioned by the suit for which you have support if partner bids it.

(Bid: 1♡)

15 ♠ A Q 6	As dealer, what vulnerable open-
♡ K 10 9 5	ing bid would you make on this
◊ K 8 6	hand, and would it make any
♣ K 9 2	difference if you were not
	vulnerable?

Answer: This is an excellent hand for a strong, i.e. vulnerable, 1NT opening. It tells partner everything in one bid, leaving you no problem as to a rebid.

Not vulnerable, you are too strong for 1NT, and there is nothing whatsoever against opening 1♡, your four-card suit. You have a stop in each suit and the right count for a rebid of 2NT if partner respond 2♣ or 2◊, or 1NT if he bids 1♠.

Compare this hand with 9, on which you had to fall back on a 'prepared' opening. This was because, with only 14 points, you were not strong enough to rebid no-trumps at the two-level.

(Bids: 1NT and 1♡)

16 ♠ K J 9 2	As dealer, whatever the score,
♡ K 8 6 5 3	would you open on this hand and,
◊ A Q 7	if so, what would you bid?
♣ 6	

Answer: Yes, with two biddable major suits and 13 points, you must open, so it only remains to consider which of the rules apply or whether it might be wiser to 'bend' one of them a bit.

If you stick to the rule of bidding your longer suit, hearts, first, you cannot possibly reverse into 2♠ if partner responds 2♣, and nor do you really want to repeat a suit which is quite as weak and straggly as your hearts. Whether you choose to open 1♡ and rebid 2♡, or open 1♠ and rebid 2♡ is something of a matter of style. But on balance I think it wiser to open 1♠, the only risk you run being that later in the auction partner may give you preference to this suit, which you don't really prefer. Compare hand 11, which illustrates a similar point.

(Bid: 1♠)

17 ♠ A K J 7   What opening bid would you
    ♡ A Q J 5 3   make on this hand?
    ◇ K 7
    ♣ 8 4

Answer: This is a very different proposition from hand 16. Here you have two good biddable suits and – even more important – a strong honour count. This means that you can afford to keep to the rule of opening the longer suit before the shorter, so you bid 1♡. You will then be able to use a forcing reverse into 2♠ if partner responds in either minor.

You will learn more about reversing in Section 4 but, in the meantime, look back to hand 16 and consider your plight if, having decided to open 1♡, partner had responded 2♣ and you had rebid 2♠. Your partner would understand this as forcing and would probably have raised to 3♠ or put you back to 3♡ – and you wouldn't like it at all! With the hand above, you would have no such reservations.

(Bid: 1♡)

18 ♠ 7   At game to your opponents you
    ♡ A Q 8 6 5 4 3   deal yourself this hand. Would you
    ◇ 9   bid and, if so, what?
    ♣ 9 7 6 4

Answer: This is an ideal hand for an opening pre-emptive bid of 3♡, the idea of which is to disrupt your opponents' bidding to the fullest possible extent.

Unfortunately your partner has not yet had a chance to bid, so he may be the one in difficulties, from which you will realise that the best position for a pre-emptive opening is third-in-hand after two passes. But in Section 2 you will learn how responder, if he has a strong hand, should cope. Meanwhile, you will have warned him of the character of your hand as well as forcing your opponents, if they want to come into the bidding, to start at what may be an uncomfortably high level. You have robbed them of bidding space, which may make it impossible for them to discover their own best contract.

(Bid: 3♡)

19 ♠ 9 7 6 4
   ♡ A Q 8 6 5 4 3
   ◇ 9
   ♣ 7

At game to your opponents, what dealer's opening bid would you make, and would it make any difference if you were third-in-hand after two passes?

Answer: This is the same hand as 18 except that the black suits have changed places. Now you have wonderful 'shape' and excellent spade support if partner, who has not yet had a chance to bid, is contemplating opening in spades. You don't want to talk him out of this so, as dealer, it is better to pass and bide your time.

Once partner has passed, showing that he lacks the values for an opening bid, there is less need to worry about talking him out of bidding spades. By opening 3♡ you might, of course, talk your opponents out of bidding spades, but it looks more as though they will be strong in the minors, if anything. It's worth the risk, so open 3♡.

(Bids: No Bid and 3♡)

20 ♠ 9 7
   ♡ A Q J 10 6 5 4 2
   ◇ A
   ♣ 8 4

As dealer, what opening bid would you make, and would the score, or your position at the table, make any difference?

Answer: Taking the second part of the question first, no, neither the score nor your position at the table would make any difference to the fact that you have a full-scale Acol strong two opening in hearts.

There are three classes of strong two but the first, of which this is an excellent example, is a hand with eight playing tricks at the suit named. Allowing for any reasonable distribution of the outstanding hearts you have seven winners in the suit which, plus the ◇ A, makes eight tricks. Strong two bids, of course, can be made in spades, hearts, and diamonds, but not in clubs.

Nor do you count points – count playing tricks.

(Bid: 2♡)

---

21 ♠ A K Q 9 8
   ♡ 8 4
   ◇ A K J 10 8 7
   ♣ –

What opening bid would you make on this hand?

Answer: This is another class of strong two opening, a powerful two-suiter on which you need to make sure of a chance to show both suits, asking for partner's preference, as even the most slender support for the one which fits his hand best is likely to produce game.

Open 2◇, the longer of your two suits, prepared to make a forcing reverse into 3♠ if partner responds 2NT (cf. hand 17). Partner will then know that you fancy your chances of making game in 4♠ or 5◇ and that your diamonds are the longer. He will either raise 3♠ to 4♠ or put you back into diamonds.

(Bid: 2◇)

---

22 ♠ A K Q 9 8
   ♡ 8 4
   ◇ –
   ♣ A K 10 9 8 7

What opening bid would you make on this hand?

Answer: It is permissible, when the predominating suit is clubs, to make a 2♣ opening when a little under strength, but this should be confined to hands on which you really have no alternative.

This hand, though just a trifle weaker than 21 (missing the ♣J) is still a powerful two-suiter. Open 2♠ intending to make your rebid in clubs. If, for example, partner responds to 2♠ with the negative 2NT, make a jump rebid of 4♣, which is forcing. Partner must either give preference to 4♠ or raise to 5♣, either of which

you should have a good chance of making once the best fit has
been found.

(Bid: 2♠)

23 ♠ A K 7 2   What opening bid would you
   ♡ A K J 10 6   make on this hand?
   ◇ –
   ♣ K 7 5 4

Answer: Just to make it clear that there are many powerful hands
which qualify for no better than a one-level opening, here is an
example. You cannot truly tell yourself that it is so constituted
that a pass from partner is likely to cost you a missed game, and
nor is it vitally urgent for you to ensure yourself a chance to show
a second suit.

Content yourself with a bid of 1♡, though being fully prepared to reverse into 2♠ on the next round, if any. Only if
partner can bid without being forced in the first place do you
want to insist on a game contract, though obviously if he can
show any signs of life, you will take strong action.

(Bid: 1♡)

24 ♠ A K 10 5 4   What opening bid would you
   ♡ A Q J 10   make on this hand?
   ◇ Q 3
   ♣ A 7

Answer: This is an example of the third class of strong two
opening, a hand which is too strong to risk a bid at the one-level
which might be passed out, so open 2♠. This gives you a sure
chance to show your hearts on the next round and, in fact, to
explore for the best final contract. In the actual event, partner
made a positive response – in hearts! – and there was no problem
about reaching the heart slam contract.

You don't count honour points when considering a strong two
opening. You count playing strength, and also take into account
the urgency of ensuring a chance to rebid, in order to express the
nature of your hand.

(Bid: 2♠)

25 ♠ A K 6
   ♡ A 10 3
   ◊ K 9 8
   ♣ A K 7 4

Whatever your position at the table, and whatever the score, what opening bid would you make on this hand?

Answer: A hand should always be opened with the strongest bid for which it qualifies, which in this case is 2NT, showing 20–22 points in a balanced hand.

As an Acol player, each bid you make will promise something and also, by reason of the fact that you made that particular bid, it can also deny the values for an even stronger bid. Just as 1NT promises an agreed point count, so 2NT promises 20–22 points, and a 2♣ opening followed by a 2NT rebid promises 23–24 points. An even strong hand of 25 or more can be shown by a 2♣ opening and a 3NT rebid.

(Bid: 2NT)

26 ♠ A 6 2
   ♡ A K 3
   ◊ 5 4 2
   ♣ A K 4 2

What opening bid would you make on this hand?

Answer: Here you have five top tricks, but you have nothing approaching 'shape' or 'playing strength'. In fact if partner can't respond under his own steam you may well end up with just the five top tricks you started with.

This is not a hand for a power announcement. Be content with a quiet 1♣ chosen, not for the sake of making a prepared bid, but because with 18 points you can afford to open one of your longest suit, whatever it is. If partner can respond at all the future will look much brighter, and you will be able to make a forcing rebid if not a direct jump to game. For example, if partner responds 1NT which, facing 1♣, shows 8–10 points, you would rebid 3 NT points.

(Bid: 1♣)

27 ♠ A K 10 8   As dealer, what opening bid would
      ♡ A Q J 10 9   you make on this hand?
      ◇ –
      ♣ A K 7 2

Answer: It wouldn't make any difference whether you were
dealer, second, third, or fourth hand as long as you were the
opening bidder – you have a full-strength opening power house
qualifying for 2♣.

It's easy to see that the rest of the points could be so
distributed that a one-bid could be passed out, and a strong two
would do nothing like justice to the hand. You need the minimum of help from partner to be sure of at least a game. The 2♣
opening bid, particularly when it is clarified by a game-forcing
suit rebid of 2♡, will tell him this – the best possible reason for
opening 2♣ and not some lesser bid.

(Bid: 2♣)

28 ♠ A Q 7   What opening bid would you
      ♡ A J 10 6   make on this hand? What differ-
      ◇ A Q   ence would it make if the ♣Q
      ♣ A Q 8 5   became the ♣9 *or* if the ♡J became
                           the ♡K?

Answer: This is an evenly-balanced collection, obviously fitted
for play in no-trumps, so you start by counting your points. Your
total is 23½ points, too strong for a 2NT opening, so you bid 2♣,
intending to rebid 2NT to show 23–24 points.

If the hand were missing the ♣Q it would fall within the range
of a 2NT opening bid and if, with the ♣Q where she is, the ♡J
became the ♡K, it would still be correct to open 2♣, though this
time with the intention of rebidding 3NT to show 25 or more
points.

(Bids: 2♣, 2NT and 2♣)

29 ♠ A K   What opening bid would you
   ♡ Q J 10 9 8 7 6 5   make on this hand?
   ◇ A K Q
   ♣ –

Answer: Believe it or not, this is an actual hand from play, and is a perfect example of a 5♡ opening bid – perfectly safe as long as partner knows his Acol!

All you need to make 6♡ a certainty is either the ace *or* king of the suit in partner's hand, even if it is only a singleton, and if by some miracle he should have both, 7♡ is equally safe. Yet you have only 19 points and if partner should turn up with 14 of the outstanding ones, which don't include either the ♡A or ♡K, you will have a hard job to keep him from bidding a slam if you've made the mistake of opening 2♣ or even 2♡.

An opening of 5♡ or 5♠ instructs responder to raise to six if he holds either the ace or king of your suit, even if it is a singleton and, with both, to raise to seven. It also tells him that none of the other cards in the pack are of any interest.

(Bid: 5♡)

30 ♠ A K Q   What opening bid would you
   ♡ A K Q   make on this hand?
   ◇ K Q J 10 9 8 7
   ♣ –

Answer: To end this section, here's another cracking big opening bid, this time a conventional 4NT, because partner's exact cards are of supreme importance. If he has the ◇A you want to play in 7◇, but even if he has a Yarborough, you want to play in 6◇.

If you open 2♣ and subsequently bid a 'Blackwood' 4NT, a 5◇ reply showing one ace would leave you guessing as to whether it were the vital ◇A or the useless ♣A. Open 4NT, which asks for the following responses – with the ◇A, ♡A, or ♠A, five of the ace suit; with the ♣A, 6♣; and with two aces, 5NT. With no ace, of course, the response is 5♣, and opener's decision after the initial response must be taken as final.

(Bid: 4NT)

Competition quiz

In competition against another player, one should answer the three questions in the **A** set, and the other the three questions in the **B** set on each page.

1A As dealer at Love All, what opening bids would you make?

1 ♠ Q J 9 6 3	2 ♠ 10 6	3 ♠ 10 6
♡ K Q 10 7 4	♡ A Q 9 8 6	♡ A Q 9 8 6 4
◇ 7	◇ 9	◇ 9 3
♣ A 3	♣ K 10 9 3 2	♣ K 10 9

Answers:

Bid (2 points) — Reason (3 points)

1   1♠   The higher-ranking of equal and adjacent suits, allowing for a safe rebid in the other.

2   No Bid   Had the suits been adjacent you could have considered opening in the higher-ranking. As it is, neither suit nor the outside strength warrants an opening bid.

3   1♡   A six-card suit, which is always *re*biddable, affords a safe sign-off rebid.

1B As dealer at Love All, what opening bids would you make?

1 ♠ Q J 9 6 3	2 ♠ 10 6	3 ♠ Q J 9 6 3
♡ 7	♡ A K J 8 6	♡ 7
◇ K Q 10 7 4	◇ A 10 7 4	◇ A 3
♣ A 3	♣ J 8	♣ K Q 10 7 4

Answers:

Bid (2 points) — Reason (3 points)

1   1♠   Too good to pass. Open 1♠ intending to rebid 2◇ if partner responds 2♣. If, however, the response is 2♡, you will have to rebid 2♠, as the hand is not good enough to show a new suit at the three-level (a one-round force).

| 2 | 1♡ | A full-strength opening hand with a safe rebid in its second suit, even though this is only a four-card one. |
| 3 | 1♣ | Now the two five-card suits are both black, and the correct opening is 1♣, leaving a safe rebid in spades if partner responds in a red suit. |

2A As dealer at Love All, what opening bids would you make?

1 ♠ K J 9 7 4	2 ♠ A K Q J	3 ♠ K J 9 7 4
♡ A Q J 10 6	♡ K J 9 7 4	♡ 9 6 3
◇ K 7	◇ 9 6 3	◇ 7
♣ 8	♣ 7	♣ A K Q J

Answers:

Bid	Reason
(2 points)	(3 points)
1 1♠	The higher-ranking of equal and adjacent suits. You must not let the heart honours go to your head, as discovering the best suit fit is far more important than the honours bonus.
2 1♠	In spite of the rule that the longer suit should be bid before the shorter, an opening of 1♡ leaves you no sensible rebid if partner responds 2♣, whereas an opening of 1♠ leaves you a rebid of 2♡. (Note that this is a matter of style – some players would prefer to open 1♡ and rebid hearts unless responder bids spades.)
3 1♠	If you open 1♣ partner will be entitled to understand from a subsequent spade bid that your clubs are at least as long as, if not longer, than your spades.

2B As dealer at Love All, what opening bids would you make?

1 ♠ K J 9 7 4	2 ♠ 9 3	3 ♠ 9 6 3
♡ 9 3	♡ K J 9 7 4	♡ K J 9 7 4
◇ 7	◇ 7	◇ 7
♣ A K Q J 10	♣ A K Q J 10	♣ A K Q J

Answers:

Bid		Reason
(2 points)		(3 points)

1   1♣ This is a simple case of two black suits of equal length. Open 1♣ leaving yourself a sensible rebid of 1♠.

2   1♣ With these two non-adjacent suits you choose to open 1♣ because the suit is good enough to rebid if partner bids 1♠. If he bids 1◊, you rebid 1♡.

3   1♡ The four-card club suit is not *re*biddable. Open 1♡ intending to rebid 2♣ over 1♠ or repeat hearts over 2◊.

3A What opening bids would you make if using a weak no-trump, and what if using a strong no-trump?

1	♠ A Q 9	2	♠ A Q 9	3	♠ A Q 9
	♡ K J 6		♡ K 8 6		♡ K J 6
	◊ Q 10 7 4		◊ Q 10 9 7 4		◊ Q 10 7
	♣ J 6 2		♣ Q 6		♣ K 10 6 2

Answers:

Bids	Reasons
(1 point each)	(1½ points each)

1   1NT if using 'weak' as this leaves you no rebid problems.

   1◊ if using 'strong', the hand is not up to standard for 1NT. The clubs don't qualify even for a 'prepared' 1♣.

2   1NT if using 'weak'. A slight compromise, as the hand contains no satisfactory rebid if you open 1◊.

   1◊ which is the only possible alternative to passing.

3   1♣ if using 'weak' – too strong for 1NT.

   1NT if using 'strong', for which it is perfectly fitted.

3B What opening bids would you make if using a weak no-trump, and what if using a strong no-trump?

1	♠ A 9 8 5	2	♠ A K 8	3	♠ K Q 7 5
	♡ K J 7		♡ K 9 7 5		♡ A J 10
	◊ Q 9 8		◊ K J 5		◊ K Q 9
	♣ K J 7		♣ J 7 4		♣ K 7 4

Answers:

Bids   Reasons
(1 point each)   (1½ points each)

1   1NT if using 'weak' – the right count and no future problems.

     1♣ if using 'strong'. With both minors qualifying, open 1♣, a 'prepared' bid with insufficient strength for 1NT.

2   1♡ if using 'weak', intending to rebid 1NT to show 15–16 points.

    1NT if using 'strong' – no need to look for any alternative.

3   1♠ in either case, as the hand is too strong for even a 'strong' no-trump. There's no need to use a 'prepared' minor, so open in your four-card suit.

4A What opening bids would you make on these 4–4–4–1 hands?

1 ♠ A J 9 8	2 ♠ 7	3 ♠ K J 8 2
♡ 7	♡ 9 8 6 3	♡ 9 8 6 3
◇ K Q 9 3	◇ A K J 7	◇ A K J 3
♣ A J 10 9	♣ A Q 10 6	♣ A

Answers:

Bid   Reason
(2 points)   (3 points)

1   1◇ The basic rule is that with three biddable suits you should open one of the suit below the singleton.

2   1◇ The hearts can't be considered biddable, so treat the hand as a diamond-club two-suiter, and open one of the higher-ranking of equal and adjacent suits.

3   1♠ Treat the hand as a spade-diamond two-suiter plus *heart* support. 1♠ is the bid best calculated to facilitate the rest of the auction.

4B What opening bids would you make on these 4–4–4–1 hands?

1 ♠ A Q 9 8	2 ♠ A Q 9 8	3 ♠ A
♡ K 10 7 6	♡ K Q 9 3	♡ K 10 7 6
◇ 5	◇ A J 10 9	◇ A Q 9 8
♣ Q 10 5 4	♣ 7	♣ Q 10 5 4

Answers:

Bid	Reason
(2 points)	(3 points)

1   No   The honour count is not good enough to compensate
      Bid   for the lack of playing strength.

2   1♡   An exception to the rule given in **4A, 1**. When the singleton is in clubs, open 1♡ which may facilitate a spade response. Failing this, there is a sensible rebid of 2◇ over 2♣ or a raise if responder bids diamonds.

3   1♡   The suit below the singleton. Note the difference from 1 in this section – the addition of the ♠A makes an opening bid mandatory.

5A   If using a 12–14 point no-trump, what opening bids would you make?

1	♠ A Q J 7	2	♠ A Q J 7	3	♠ A Q J 7
	♡ A K 9 2		♡ J 8 3		♡ 7 4
	◇ J 8 5		◇ A K 9 2		◇ A K 9 2
	♣ 7 4		♣ 7 4		♣ J 8 5

Answers:

Bid	Reason
(2 points)	(3 points)

1   1♡   4–4–3–2 hands which don't qualify for a no-trump opening can be more difficult to bid than 4–4–4–1 hands. Here, however, you simply bid the lower-ranking of equal and adjacent suits.

2   1◇   Open 1◇, and if the response is 2♣, rebid 2NT.

3   1◇   The same hand except that now the support is for clubs. 1◇–1♡–1♠ is sensible, but what do you rebid if you open 1♠ and responder bids 2♡?

5B   If using a 12–14 point no-trump, what opening bids would you make?

1	♠ 7 4	2	♠ A Q J 7	3	♠ J 8 3
	♡ A Q J 7		♡ J 8 3		♡ A Q J 7
	◇ J 8 5		◇ 7 4		◇ 7 4
	♣ A K 9 2		♣ A K 9 2		♣ A K 9 2

Answers:

Bid		Reason
(2 points)		(3 points)

1 1♣ Open 1♣ and rebid 1NT. There is no need to worry about the quality of the diamond stop at the one-level.

2 1♣ This opening is conditioned by nothing except the fact that, with two black suits of equal length, you should open 1♣.

3 1♣ If partner responds 1◇ you can rebid 1♡ and if instead he responds 1♠ you are not over-stating your hand if you rebid 1NT. Note that none of the six hands on this page is strong enough to show a new suit at the three-level (1♡–2◇–3♣) which is a one-round force.

6A Using a 12–14 point no-trump, what opening bids would you make?

1 ♠ A J 8	2 ♠ A K 8	3 ♠ 9 6 5 2
♡ A Q 6 5 3	♡ A Q 7 5	♡ K Q 6
◇ K 9 8	◇ K J 6 2	◇ A K 8
♣ 7 5	♣ A 8	♣ A J 8

Answers:

Bid		Reason
(2 points)		(3 points)

1 1♡ Although within the limits for a weak no-trump opening, this hand is far better expressed by a 1♡ opening and, if expedient, a heart rebid.

2 2NT A perfect hand for this bid, showing 20–22 points and an even distribution.

3 1♠ With 17 points this hand is strong enough to open with one of the four-card suit, even if it is a pretty poor one.

6B Using a 12–14 point no-trump, what opening bids would you make?

1 ♠ 10 9 8	2 ♠ A K 8	3 ♠ A Q
♡ A 8 7 5	♡ A Q 7 5	♡ A Q 7
◇ K J 6	◇ K 9 6 2	◇ A Q 9 8 5
♣ A K 3	♣ 9 8	♣ K J 8

Answers:

Bid (2 points)		Reason (3 points)
1	1♣	Too good for a weak no-trump, the alternative opening is 1♡. If responder bids 2♣ or 2◊, rebid 1NT, hoping that partner has a spade stop.
2	1♡	Treat the hand as a straightforward red two-suiter, and open one of the higher-ranking of equal and adjacent suits.
3	2NT	There's no law against opening 2NT with a five-card suit. Besides coming within the prescribed 20–22 points, this tenace-studded collection is likely to play better with the lead coming up to, rather than through it.

7A Using a 15–17 point no-trump, what opening bids would you make, and what if you were using a 12–14 point no-trump?

1 ♠ A 9 8	2 ♠ A J 9	3 ♠ A Q 9
♡ K J 7 2	♡ K J 7 2	♡ K J 7 2
◊ 9 8 5	◊ Q 8 5	◊ K 9 3
♣ A Q 6	♣ A 7 6	♣ A Q 6

Answers:

Bids (1 point each)		Reasons (1½ points each)
1	1♣	Too weak for a 'strong' no-trump so open a 'prepared' 1♣.
	1NT	if using 'weak', and in spite of the diamond weakness.
2	1NT	'strong', for which you have the perfect hand.
	1♡	if using 'weak'. No need for a 'prepared' opening as with something in every suit you can rebid 2NT if responder bids 2♣ or 2◊, and 1NT if he bids 1♠.
3	1♡	in either case, as the hand is too strong for any variety of no-trump. Bid one of the four-card suit and let the future take care of itself.

7B Using a 15–17 point no-trump, what opening bids would you make, and what if you were using a 12–14 point no-trump?

1 ♠ A 9 8	2 ♠ A J 9 7 2	3 ♠ A Q 9
♡ K J 7 2	♡ K J 2	♡ K J 7 2
◇ A Q 6	◇ Q 8	◇ K 10 8 4
♣ 9 8 5	♣ A 7 6	♣ 6 2

Answers:

Bids	Reasons
(1 point each)	(1½ points each)

1   1◇   Not good enough for a 'strong' no-trump. Bid 1◇, *not* 1♣, as you have no high honour in the latter.

        1NT   in spite of the club weakness. It's the most preemptive of the one-level bids as well as leaving no rebid problems.

2   1♠   in either case as there is nothing against this perfectly natural opening which will not cause a rebid problem.

3   1♡   in both cases. Below the range for a 'strong' no-trump, simply treat it as a red two-suiter.

        1NT   Use the most pre-emptive one-bid available.

8A What opening bids would you make on these hands?

1 ♠ A K Q 10 8 5 3	2 ♠ A K J 10 9 6	3 ♠ A J 9 8 5 3 2
♡ K Q 4	♡ A Q J 10 5	♡ K Q 4
◇ 6	◇ K 3	◇ 6
♣ K 3	♣ –	♣ K 3

Answers:

Bid	Reason
(2 points)	(3 points)

1   2♠   Allowing for any reasonable break, this hand contains eight playing tricks at spades – a strong two. Do note that playing strength is more relevant than point-count when choosing a bid for these hands.

2   2♠   Another type of strong two, a powerful two-suiter, on which it is vital to ensure a second chance to bid.

3   1♠   Good as it is, this hand lacks the power required for a

strong two. Open 1♠ prepared to rebid strongly if
partner can make any unforced response.

8B   What opening bids would you make on these hands?

	1 ♠ A Q J 9 6 4	2 ♠ 8	3 ♠ A K
	♡ 8	♡ A Q J 10 9	♡ A Q J 10 7 5 4
	◇ –	◇ A K 10 7 4	◇ 6 2
	♣ A K J 8 3 2	♣ 10 5	♣ K 3

Answers:

Bid	Reason
(2 points)	(3 points)

1   2♠   With a hand worth a strong two you can't bid 2♣
           which would, of course, be conventional. Open 2♠
           and make your rebid in clubs.

2   1♡   Not good enough for more than a one-bid. Open 1♡
           and await developments.

3   2♡   A strong single-suited hand on which you can count a
           sure eight tricks if played in hearts.

9A   At equal vulnerability, what dealer's opening bid would
you make, and would you make the same bid third-in-hand
after two passes?

	1 ♠ A Q 9 7 6 4 3	2 ♠ 6	3 ♠ K Q J 10 9 6 3 2
	♡ 8 5	♡ J 8 5 3	♡ –
	◇ 6 2	◇ A Q 9 7 6 4 3	◇ 6 2
	♣ J 5	♣ 5	♣ A 9 2

Answers:

Bids	Reasons
(1 point each)	(1½ points each)

1   3♠   as dealer. A hand with no defensive values, though
           3♠ may interfere with the enemy's bidding
           sequence.

     3♠   as third-in-hand. Nothing has changed except that
           fourth-in-hand may be prevented from bidding.

2   No   as dealer. Don't warn partner off showing hearts, for
     Bid which you have excellent support.

     3◇   as third-in-hand after partner's pass. It is now less

likely that you have a good heart contract available, and obstruction of the opposition may be given priority.

3   2♠   as dealer, a normal strong two opening bid.

     4♠   as third-in-hand, showing a maximum of two defensive tricks and obstructing any red suit attempt by your opponents.

9B At equal vulnerability, what dealer's opening bid would you make, and would you make the same bid third-in-hand after two passes?

1	♠ 7	2	♠ 6	3	♠ 8
	♡ A Q J 10 8 7 6 3		♡ 7		♡ K J 10 9 7 6 3 2
	◇ A 7 2		◇ K 5 4		◇ 7 5 4
	♣ 6		♣ A K J 8 6 5 4 3		♣ 6

Answers:

Bids	Reasons
(1 point each)	(1½ points each)

1   2♡   as dealer, with eight playing tricks at hearts – a strong two.

     4♡   as third-in-hand after two passes. You have no hopes of a slam for your side, and obstruction of the opposition is now of great importance.

2   5♣   as dealer, with a long strong suit and absolutely no defence in either major.

     5♣   as third-in-hand for the same reasons.

3   3♡   as dealer. No other suit interests you and you want to put a pre-emptive barrier in the path of the enemy.

     3♡   as third-in-hand for the same reason.

10A What opening bids would you make?

1	♠ A K 6 4	2	♠ A Q J 4	3	♠ A K 6 4
	♡ K 10		♡ A J 6		♡ A 6 4
	◇ A K 9 3		◇ K Q 4		◇ A 9 3
	♣ A Q 7		♣ A K Q		♣ A 7 2

Answers:

Bid	Reason
(2 points)	(3 points)

1   2♣   This is clearly a no-trump type hand, but as an opening of 2NT shows 20–22 points *only*, here a stronger bid is needed. Open 2♣, intending to rebid 2NT to show 23–24 points.

2   2♣   This hand is even stronger, and too good for 2♣ with a 2NT rebid. Open 2♣ intending to rebid 3NT to show 25 or more points.

3   1♠   19 points, not strong enough for better than a one-level bid, as it has no 'playing strength'. Open 1♠ and await developments. You can always force on the next round – if any.

10B   What opening bids would you make?

1	♠ A Q	2	♠ A 9 8	3	♠ A J 10
	♡ A K 9 2		♡ K Q 9 7		♡ K Q 9 7
	◇ A 9 8 7		◇ A K 6		◇ A K 6
	♣ K Q 10		♣ K 6 3		♣ A K 3

Answers:

Bid	Reason
(2 points)	(3 points)

1   2NT   In addition to showing 20–22 points, this bid will also tell responder how little help you need for a successful game contract. Believe it or not, but at a duplicate event, one player chose a 'prepared' 1♣ and had only herself to blame when this was passed out. Responder had ♠K–x–x and ♣J–9–x–x.

2   1♡   Just below strength for 2NT. Open one of the four-card suit, *not* 1♣, which should only be used when the hand otherwise lacks a sensible re-bid.

3   2♣   Too strong for 2NT, so open 2♣ intending to rebid 2NT.

11A What opening bids would you make on these hands?

1 ♠ K J 6 3	2 ♠ A K Q 7 5	3 ♠ A K Q J 6
♡ A K J 10 4	♡ A K 9	♡ A 9
◇ −	◇ 6	◇ A
♣ A Q 7 2	♣ K Q J 4	♣ K J 9 8 4

Answers:

Bid		Reason
(2 points)		(3 points)

1   1♡   Below strength for better than a one-level bid. Open in your longest suit, prepared to take strong action if partner can bid at all.

2   2♣   23+ points, allowing for the singleton. Don't leave partner guessing by making any lesser bid.

3   2♠   Just below strength for 2♣, which would be conventional, but too good for a one-level bid which might be passed out. A strong two opening will ensure a chance to show both suits and hear partner's preference.

11B What opening bids would you make on these hands?

1 ♠ A K J 10 6 4	2 ♠ A K J 10 6 4	3 ♠ A K J 10 6 4
♡ A Q	♡ A 8	♡ A Q
◇ K Q 9	◇ K 9 8	◇ A K 8
♣ 7 3	♣ 7 3	♣ 7 3

Answers:

Bid		Reason
(2 points)		(3 points)

1   2♠   Far too good for a one-level opening which might be passed out. Tell partner how little help you need for a successful game contract.

2   1♠   Short of the values for a stronger opening. You can always bid strongly on the next round if partner can respond.

3   2♣   All the qualifications for this strongest opening bid. You open 2♣ to tell partner how good your hand is. As little as the ◇Q in partner's hand plus a 'lucky' heart lead would give you a game.

12A What opening bids would you make on these hands?

1 ♠ Q J 10 9 8 7 6 5	2 ♠ A K J 7	3 ♠ A 6
♡ –	♡ 7 3	♡ A K J 10 7
◇ A K	◇ –	◇ A J 8
♣ A K Q	♣ A K Q J 10 7 6	♣ K Q 6

Answers:

Bid	Reason
(2 points)	(3 points)

1   5♠   A conventional opening bid (in the majors only) asking partner to bid the small slam if he has either the ♠A *or* ♠K, even if singleton. With both he must bid the grand slam and with neither, however good the rest of his hand, he must pass.

2   2♣   Although slightly under strength, it is permissible to open 2♣ when the predominating suit is clubs.

3   2♣   Great playing strength. Tell partner this so that he can judge the worth of even a few points opposite.

12B What opening bids would you make on these hands?

1 ♠ –	2 ♠ A 6	3 ♠ K Q J 10 7 5
♡ K Q J 10 6	♡ A Q J 8 7	♡ 8
◇ A	◇ –	◇ A K Q
♣ A K Q J 10 8 6	♣ K Q J 10 7 4	♣ A K Q

Answers:

Bid	Reason
(2 points)	(3 points)

1   4NT   Conventional, requesting partner to name his ace or aces, if any. If he has the worthless ♠A you will play in 6♣, but if he has the ♡A you can bid the grand slam.

2   2♡   Although the predominating suit is clubs, it is not necessary to devalue a 2♣ opening when there is an alternative bid available.

3   2♣   A small slam requires at least one major suit ace from partner, failing which you can play quietly in 4♠. If the bidding starts 2♣–2◇, you will rebid a conventional 3♠ to ask if he has any one ace at all.

Section 2

First Round Responding Bids

The basic rules

A response in a new suit to a suit opening bid is forcing for one round *unless* the responder has previously passed, a fact which may make a difference to responder's choice of bid. Both no-trump and suit limit-bids are available, and these show both the upper and lower limits of the values held, leaving responder under no obligation to bid again unless his partner forces him to do so. In principle, a suit limit-bid promises four-card trump support, but there are occasions when this rule has to give way to common sense.

1 *Change of suit:*

1♡–1♠ or 1◇–1♠	At the one-level, 6+ points with a biddable four-card or longer suit. Forcing for one round unless responder has previously passed. Promises no more strength than 1NT would do.
1♡–2◇ or 1◇–2♣	At the two-level, a minimum of 8 points. Stronger responding hand will be shown on the next round.
1♡–3◇ or 1♡–2♠	A jump of one level more than is necessary is strength-showing and forcing to game. Either a good quality suit or possibly a short suit with good support for opener's suit, or an evenly-balanced 16 or more points.

1♡–3♠ or 1◇–4♠	A jump of two or more levels is pre-emptive, showing weakness except for the suit bid, which will be long. Used to obstruct the opponents' bidding to the full and also to warn partner of the character of the hand.
1♡–4♣	Swiss convention, showing four-card support for partner's major suit opening, two aces, and 13–15 points.
1♠–4◇	Swiss convention, showing four-card support for partner's major suit opening, three aces and 13–15 points. Both 4♣ and 4◇ deny the strength for an immediate force. There are other versions of Swiss.

2 *Suit limit-bids:*

1♠–2♠	Weak, showing 6–9 points with four-card trump support.
1♡–3♡	Showing four-card trump support, good 'shape', and 10–12 points including distribution. Strong and encouraging though not forcing.
1◇–3◇	In the minors, denies ability to bid more constructively, showing at least 10–12 points, and four-card trump support. Suggests a possible 3NT contract. Again, highly encouraging though not forcing.

3 *No-trump limit-bids:*

1♠–1NT	In response to a major suit opening shows 6–9 points in a hand lacking four-card trump support. A weak 'keep open' bid.
1♣–1NT	A more positive bid, showing 8–10 points, as all other suits are available for a one-level response.
1♡–2NT	In response to any suit opening shows 11–12 points in a balanced hand. Encouraging but not forcing.

1♠–3NT   In response to any suit opening shows 13–15 points in a balanced hand. Not to be taken as a 'stop' bid. Avoid this response if an alternative is available, as it can hamper possible slam investigations.

4 *Responses to strong two openings:*

2◇, 2♡,   Strong two opening bids are unconditionally forc-
2♠   ing for one round, with a negative response of 2NT if you have less than 4 points.

2♡–3♡   Single raise of suit opened shows adequate trump support and at least one ace or void. Unlimited in strength and allowing space for slam investigations.

2♠–4♠   A double jump to the four-level in either major or
or   minor shows adequate trump support, about 8–10
2◇–4◇   points and *no* first-round control (i.e. no ace or void).

2♡–3NT   About 10–12 points, no void, and trump fit too poor for direct raise to the four-level.

2◇–2♡   At least a four-card biddable suit and 8 or more points, too good for a 2NT negative when the suit can be shown cheaply at the two-level.

2♡–3◇   When the bidding level must be raised, shows at least a five-card biddable suit and 9 or more points, and denies sufficient support for opener's suit to give a direct raise.

2♡–3♠   A jump take-out in a new suit shows a long, strong and solid suit, at least as good as A–K–Q–J to six or A–K–Q to seven.

5 *Responses to 2♣ openings:*

2♣   The 2♣ opening bid is unconditionally forcing to game unless opener rebids 2NT.

2◇   Is the first negative response, showing weakness, and less than the values set out overleaf.

2NT	Is the second negative if responder is still unable to make any constructive bid after opener's rebid.
2♡, 2♠, 3♣ or 3♢	Positive responses showing a biddable suit (possibly only a four-card suit at the two-level) and a minimum holding of: One ace and one king A biddable suit Any eight points.
2NT	Shows any of the above requirements but no biddable suit.

6 *Responses to pre-emptive opening bids:*

3♡–4♡	Raise to game on not less than 3–4 honour tricks and some trump fit.
3♢–4♠	Take out into a game contract on strength and own long strong suit.
3♡–3♠	Take-out into a major suit below game level is a one-round force, and opener may raise to game in responder's suit on as little as Q–x in support.
3♡–4♣	Take-out into a minor is also a one-round force and is conveniently used to agree opener's suit as trumps with a possible slam in mind.
3♠–3NT	is to play, inferring fit with opener's suit and/or long suit of own with outside controls.

7 *Responses to conventional openings:*

5 of a major	Pass unless holding either the ace *or* king of the suit opened. Raise to small slam with either, even if singleton, and to grand slam with both.
6 of a minor	Pass unless holding either the ace *or* king of the suit opened. Raise to grand slam with either, even if singleton.
4NT	With no ace, 5♣; with ♣A, 6♣; with ◇A, ♡A or ♠A, five of the ace-suit; with any two aces, 5NT.

Exercises

1 ♠ K 9 7 2
♡ 8 4
◇ Q 9 8 5
♣ 10 6 3

Your partner deals and opens 1♠.
What would you respond?

Answer: A basic rule for Acol bidding is that if a hand contains the requirements for a limit-bid in response to partner's major suit opening, that bid is to be preferred to any other. So on the hand above there is no possible response except 2♠.

A limit-bid, though it may be highly encouraging, is never forcing. It tells partner all you have in one simple bid and leaves him to judge whether your combined forces are now worth another try. A single raise, as in this instance, is a very weak response, showing between 6–9 points, honour plus distributional. One point for the doubleton heart brings this hand up to 6 points, just worth a raise, if only for the pre-emptive value against fourth-in-hand.

(Bid: 2♠)

2 ♠ K 9 7
♡ J 8 4
◇ Q 9 8 5
♣ 10 6 3

Your partner deals and opens 1♠.
What would you respond?

Answer: One of the basic requirements for a limit-bid in partner's suit is four-card trump support, and though there are occasions when you have to break this rule, this is not one of them. In other words, if there is a sensible alternative, use it.

When partner opens 1♠ this hand is just too good to pass, but you have only three spades and no suit of your own you can bid at the one-level, let alone the two-level. Keep the bidding open with 1NT, which again shows 6–9 points, though this time it *denies* four-card trump support.

(Bid: 1NT)

3 ♠ K 9 5   Your partner deals and opens 1♡.
   ♡ A 9 2   What would you respond?
   ◊ K 9 8 6 4
   ♣ 8 3

Answer: Lacking four-card heart support you look first for a response other than a direct raise in hearts, as it is always unwise to make a misleading bid if a truthful one can be found.

The minimum count required for a change-of-suit response at the two-level is 8 points, and here you have 10, plus a biddable diamond suit. Bid 2◊ which will tell partner that you are not strong enough to make a game-forcing bid, that you either lack four-card heart support or are too strong to risk an immediate raise to 3♡ which might be passed, and that your hand is not sufficiently evenly-balanced for you to be looking for a no-trump contract at this stage.

(Bid: 2◊)

4 ♠ Q 9 8   Your partner deals and opens 1♡.
   ♡ 9 7 6 2   What would you respond, and
   ◊ 7   what would you have responded if
   ♣ A 9 6 4 2   his opening bid had been 1♠?

Answer: In the first case you have no problem. In support of a 1♡ opening you have 6 honour points, 2 distributional points (the diamond singleton) and four-card trump support – tailor-made for a limit-bid of 2♡.

When the opening bid is 1♠, however, you lack four-card trump support, and nor have you got the 8 points you would promise by a change-of-suit to 2♣. Since with 6 points you can't possibly pass, you might consider the keep-open bid of 1NT but this, with your singleton diamond, would hardly be realistic. The least of the available evils is to raise 1♠ to 2♠. After all, you have three spades to an honour and a useful 'ruffing value'.

(Bids: 2♡ and 2♠)

5 ♠ K J 6   What would you respond to your
   ♡ Q 10 8 5   partner's opening 1♠, and what to
   ◊ K 10 9 8 5   his opening 1♡?
   ♣ 6

Answer: A perfectly natural change-of-suit bid of 2♦ is the correct response to 1♠. Clearly you shouldn't raise spades when you have a sensible alternative, and to bid in no-trumps would be quite unrealistic.

The situation is very different when partner opens 1♡. Now you have excellent four-card trump support as well as the necessary 10–12 points (honours + distribution) for a limit-bid of 3♡. This, as well as telling partner both the upper and lower limits of your values in one simple bid, is also highly pre-emptive, and may make it impossible for your left-hand opponent to come into the auction at all.

(Bids: 2♦ and 3♡)

6	♠ A 10 7 5 4 2	What would you respond to your
	♡ 7	partner's opening 1♡, and what
	♦ Q 10 8	difference would it make if your
	♣ 7 5 4	spade suit were exchanged with
		your clubs?

Answer: The first question is easily disposed of – you would bid 1♠ which promises no more than a bid of 1NT would do, except that it shows a biddable spade suit.

Mentally exchanging your two black suits, you can't support hearts so your choice, since you can't consider passing, is between 1NT, for which you have the right count but not the 'shape', and 2♣, for which you have the shape but not the count! The best choice here is 1NT.

(Bids: 1♠ and 1NT)

7	♠ A Q 8	Your partner deals and opens 1♦.
	♡ 9 3 2	What would you respond?
	♦ J 9 7 6	
	♣ 10 9 8	

Answer: The limit-bids, that is, the direct raises in partner's bid suit, are just as much available in the minors as in the majors. But there is this difference – five of a minor for a game is a long way to go when 3NT may be an easier contract. The actual values required for a direct minor suit raise to either the two or the three-level are the same as for the major suits but, particularly when you have not previously passed, you should make sure there is no possibly more constructive bid you can make.

On this hand there is nothing you can honestly do except raise 1 ◇ to 2 ◇. Your only possible alternative is 1NT, but your partner will have at least three diamonds to a high honour, and probably more. To know that you have four diamonds in a weak hand won't deter him from bidding on if he himself is strong.

(Bid: 2 ◇)

8	♠ A 10 8 6	Your partner deals and opens 1 ◇.
	♡ K 8 7 2	What would you respond, and
	◇ J 10 8	would it make any difference if
	♣ 9 3	your 9♣ were the ♣A?

Answer: Holding two four-card suits in a weak hand worth only one forward-going move, it is better to respond in the lower-ranking first, which is best calculated to facilitate the rest of the auction. An exception to this is when the lower-ranking suit is too weak to suggest as trumps which would be the case if, for instance, your ♡K and 9♣ were exchanged for the 9♡ and ♣K. The correct response as the hand is, is 1♡.

If you added the ♣A, four more honour points, the hand becomes worth at least a second forward move, but the best response would still be 1♡.

(Bids: 1♡ in either case)

9	♠ A Q 8	Your partner deals and opens 1 ◇.
	♡ Q 9 8 6	What would you respond, and
	◇ J 9 8 7	would it make any difference if
	♣ 6 3	you had dealt and passed
		originally?

Answer: When you have not previously passed you should make what may possibly be a constructive bid of 1♡. This is, after all, a one-round force, so if it doesn't help partner into a no-trump contract, there will always be time to put him back into diamonds.

If you had dealt and passed originally, your change of suit to 1♡ would no longer be forcing and partner, with a reasonable three-card heart fit, might well pass when the hand belongs in diamonds. It, therefore, becomes far wiser to settle for a limit-bid of 3 ◇ because of the risk that you may never get a chance to put partner back to this suit.

(Bids: 1 ♡ and 3 ◇)

10	♠ Q 8 7	Your partner deals and opens 1♣.
	♡ Q 9 8	What would you respond? Would
	◇ J 9 8 7	it make any difference if your
	♣ J 8 3	spades were ♠A–Q–8 instead of
		♠Q–8–7?

Answer: With the hand as it is you should respond 1 ◇ to partner's 1♣ because – and this is the important point – you are not strong enough to respond 1NT to a 1♣ opening.

With the other three suits all available for a one-level response, or even perhaps a raise of 1♣ to 2♣ if that is your only four-card suit, Acol players keep a response of 1NT to 1♣ as a positive bid showing 8–10 points, not the mere 6–9 points it would show in response to any other suit.

With the spades topped up by the ♠A you could, it is true, still respond 1 ◇, but it is a far more constructive bid to show that your count, without any good biddable suit, is 8–10 points, so in this second situation 1NT would be the best response.

(Bids: 1 ◇ and 1NT)

11	♠ K J 6	Your partner deals and opens 1♠.
	♡ J 9 5	What would you respond, and
	◇ Q 9 8 5	would it make any difference if
	♣ A 8 5	you had dealt and passed
		originally?

Answer: Limit-bids in the major suits or in no-trumps are not affected in any way by your position at the table though they can, of course, be affected by intervening bids. Here there is no intervention to contend with. Not strong enough to open, though with one more point you could have opened a 12–14 point no-trump if no one had spoken before you, you have, whether you've already had the chance to pass or not, a perfect limited response of 2NT. This tells partner in the one single bid that you have an evenly-balanced hand of 11–12 points, and no five-card suit.

(Bids: 2NT in either case)

12 ♠ K J 6		Your partner deals and opens 1♡.
♡ J 9 5		What would you respond?
◊ Q 9 8 5		
♣ A Q 5		

Answer: You will note that you are not asked what you would respond if you had previously passed because you would, of course, have opened on this hand, either 1NT or 1♣ according to the strength of the no-trump being used.

Just occasionally hands crop up on which the only sensible response is an immediate 3NT. This shows 13–15 points and obviously partner, with a strong opening hand, must take it as encouragement to go on rather than as a 'stop' bid. However, bidding on can be difficult at the high level reached, for which reason it is a response to be avoided if a more constructive one can be found. Here there is no more constructive alternative available and it is, in fact, a typical hand for the bid.

(Bid: 3NT)

13 ♠ J 9 7 5 4		At Game to your opponents your
♡ 8 3		partner deals and opens 1♠. Your
◊ 9		right hand opponent passes – what
♣ K Q 10 8 5		would you bid?

Answer: An intervening bid on your right hand would, in fact, make no difference. The best thing you can do, particularly at the score, is to jump direct to 4♠. This is a highly pre-emptive measure, designed to make life as difficult as possible for your left-hand opponent who, if he wants to bid, will now be forced to start his operations at a very high level. He may, in consequence, be quite unable to discover his own best spot – or even if he has one!

In the early days of the Acol System, this direct jump to the four-level was used as a limit-bid, even stronger than a bid at the three-level. Nowadays, however, there is other machinery available for the strong hands, and the four-level bid is purely pre-emptive. Trump fit and distribution are the clues.

(Bid: 4♠)

14 ♠ 9
   ♡ 6 5
   ◊ K Q 10 8 6
   ♣ Q J 10 8 3

At Game to your opponents your partner deals and opens 1◊. Your right hand opponent passes – what would you bid?

Answer: Trump support, 'shape', and above all, no defence what-soever in the majors, make this hand suitable for a pre-emptive jump to 4◊. As in hand 13, note the useful club side suit.

Weakness, particularly in the majors, is an essential for this bid which, of course, precludes any chance of your side playing in 3NT. So if partner wants to go on to game, it will have to be in diamonds, though he is at liberty to pass the four-level bid if he thinks fit. Whichever he chooses, he will know that he is facing weakness, though that he can at least be sure of trump length in your hand.

(Bid: 4◊)

15 ♠ 9 6
   ♡ K 9 8 5
   ◊ A Q 9 2
   ♣ K J 10

Your partner deals and opens 1♡. What would you respond?

Answer: Thinking back to hand 5 in this section, you may have considered a 3♡ limit-bid, but this shows, in addition to the minimum of four-card trump support, a count of 10–12 points, *no more*. Furthermore, a limit-bid, even at this encouragingly high level, is not forcing. Partner could pass and, facing your powerful hand, a game might well be missed, let alone a slam if he happens to be strong for his bid.

The answer is to use a delayed game raise, that is a change of suit bid as your immediate response, and then a jump bid to game level on the next round, whether partner merely rebids his hearts or not. This will show him that you were too strong for a limit-bid whilst, of course, not quite strong enough for a forcing take-out.

(Bid: 2◊)

16 ♠ 9 6   Your partner deals and opens 1♡.
   ♡ A 9 8 5   What would you respond?
   ◊ A Q 9 2
   ♣ A 10 9

Answer: This hand differs from 15 in that the four points in clubs are the ace instead of the K–J, yet this makes all the difference to the best response.

The Swiss convention, which allows the pin-pointing of controls as well as giving the assurance of four-card trump support, is the answer this time. There are various versions of this convention, so it's as well to be sure that you and your partner are using the same one. But the one advocated in *All About Acol* uses an immediate response of 4♣ to partner's major suit opening bid to show two aces, four-card trump support, and 13–15 points. 4◊ shows the same trump support and three aces, again with 13–15 points. We shall see how the bidding develops after that in later sections but, meanwhile, respond 4◊ on this hand, not because you have a diamond suit, but because you have a specific holding whilst wanting to insist on at least a game contract.

(Bid: 4◊)

17 ♠ Q 9 6   Your partner deals and opens 1♠.
   ♡ K 6   What would you respond?
   ◊ A Q 7
   ♣ A Q 9 7 5

Answer: You are far too strong for anything other than an immediate game force of 3♣. The ♠Q–x–x is anything but a misfit and in any case, whatever the final denomination, you already know that the hand must be played in at least a game, if not a slam.

When making a forcing take-out choose, if possible, a suit in which you have first-round control and also, provided you are willing to play in partner's bid suit, one which ranks below his. This is not always possible, but bear these two principles in mind. Also, and this is equally important, once you have made your force, don't insist on bidding on to a slam unless you have extra concealed strength in your hand. After all, you will already have said 'game certain, slam possible', a hint which partner should be able to take unless his hand is near minimum.

(Bid: 3♣)

18 ♠ Q 9 6 4   Your partner deals and opens 1♠.
    ♡ A 7 3   What would you respond, and
    ◊ A Q 10 8 2   would it make any difference if
    ♣ 7   your 7♡ became the ♡K?

Answer: As the hand is now it contains a perfect 4♣ Swiss bid, four-card spade support, two aces, and 13–15 points.

Add the ♡K, and it would be too strong for a Swiss response, even though it would still contain the specific holdings promised by the 4♣ bid. The correct response would be 3◊.

You will see that each response has its alloted place, not taking the place of any other. The limit-bids either in no-trumps or the suit opened show certain strength whilst denying anything more, the Swiss bids show specific holdings and demand at least a game contract whilst denying the strength to force, and so on.

(Bid: 4♣ and 3◊)

19 ♠ K 9 8 4   Your partner deals and opens 2♠,
    ♡ A Q 10 7 3   an Acol strong two. What would
    ◊ 9 3   you respond?
    ♣ 9 7

Answer: When partner opens with a strong two and you are in agreement with him that this will make a good trump suit, in other words, when you have a trump fit, immediate support is by far the most likely response to help him. Obviously, it doesn't really matter if he has one long suit or is two-suited – you are with him in the first bid suit. Tell him so by the appropriate raise, in this case a single raise to 3♠ which, in addition to promising good (not necessarily four-card) trump support, also shows 'positive' values and at least one ace or void.

Opener, with this much knowledge, can now settle for a mere game contract or take further steps towards investigating a possible slam. So here support spades, and don't show the hearts first.

(Bid: 3♠)

20 ♠ K 9 8 4   Your partner deals and opens 2♠,
    ♡ K Q J 7 3   an Acol strong two. What would
    ◊ 9 3   you respond?
    ♣ 9 7

Answer: This hand has exactly the same number of points and the same excellent spade support as in 19, but there is one important difference, and that is that it has no first-round controls, either aces or voids, even though it has the values for a positive response.

You can tell partner all this by bidding an immediate 4♠, from which he will know that, if he has any ideas of bidding a slam, he will have to provide at least three first-round controls himself.

Note the difference – a single raise is unlimited, merely agreeing trumps and promising at least one ace or void. A double raise also promises trump support but denies an ace or void.

(Bid: 4♠)

21 ♠ K 10 8 6 5   Your partner deals and opens 2♡,
    ♡ 10 8 5 2   an Acol strong two. What would
    ◊ J 6   you respond?
    ♣ 9 6

Answer: You must, at this stage, deny the values for a 'positive' response by giving the negative answer of 2NT. If you raise 2♡ to 3♡ you would be promising at least one ace or void and if you raise direct to 4♡, as in hand 20, you would promise at least a trick somewhere, even if it were not an ace or void. After all, your partner won't pass your 2NT, so even if he turns out to be two-suited, not single-suited in hearts, you will have a chance to put him back to hearts, for which you have excellent support. In fact you would certainly put him to 4♡ if he merely rebid 3♡ over your 2NT. Part of the reason for opening a strong two is to tell partner what a good hand you have, and how little help you need to make a game.

(Bid: 2NT)

22 ♠ K 10 9 2   Your partner deals and opens 2◊,
   ♡ Q J 3   an Acol strong two. What would
   ◊ 9 8   you respond, and would it make
   ♣ K J 10 7   any difference if he had opened 2♡
                     or 2♠ instead?

Answer: When partner bids 2◊ you can't do that most helpful thing, agree trumps, and nor have you a suit really good enough to wish to suggest as an alternative. You are also much too good to give a 'negative' response, and the correct bid is 3NT, which is the approximate equivalent of a 2NT limit-bid facing a one-level opening except that, in this case, it denies an ace or void.

If partner had opened 2♡ or 2♠ you would raise direct to four in either suit. You don't need four-card support for a suit good enough to be opened at the two-level, and though you have this in spades, ♡Q–J–x is more than adequate (Q–x–x would be amply good enough) in hearts.

(Bids: 3NT, 4♡ and 4♠)

23 ♠ K 9 8 3   Your partner deals and opens 1♡.
   ♡ J 10 8   What would you respond and
   ◊ 8 7 6   what difference would it make if
   ♣ 10 4 3   he had opened 2♡?

Answer: With only four points and no 'shape' whatsoever, there's only one thing you can sensibly do when partner opens at the one-level, and that's say No Bid. Even had he opened 1♠, for which you have at least a four-card fit, the lower the contract the better from your point of view.

When partner opens 2♡ you have no option. This bid is forcing for one round, so you would have to bid the 'negative' 2NT.

If anyone ever tells you it is stupid to keep a strong two open even for one round on a near Yarborough, remember that partner may have game 'cold' in his own hand and, if he can't rely on you to let him have his chance to bid it, he will be forced into devaluing his 2♣ openings on any occasion when a second chance to bid is essential to him.

(Bids: No Bid and 2NT)

24 ♠ K 9 7 2   Your partner deals and opens 2♣.
   ♡ Q 5 4   What would you respond?
   ◊ 9
   ♣ 10 9 8 5 4

Answer: This conventional opening bid is the announcement of an extremely powerful hand, though at this stage you don't know whether it is of no-trump type or based on one or more good suits. For the moment this is not your concern – you will learn more when you have heard your partner's rebid.

In the meantime your correct response is 2◊, for no other reason than that you have such a poor hand that you can only make a negative response.

When it comes to making a positive response you will find a good deal of common sense applies, as it will when a possible rebid is in question. For the moment, however, just keep the bidding open and await developments.

(Bid: 2◊)

25 ♠ Q 8 5   Your partner deals and opens 2♣.
   ♡ K Q 10 7 5   What would you respond and
   ◊ J 5   would it make any difference if
   ♣ 10 4 2   your red suits were exchanged?

Answer: With the hand as it is when partner opens 2♣ your biddable heart suit, headed by two honours and with the outside value of the ♠Q makes it worth a positive response of 2♡. This, as you can see, doesn't promise a very great deal, and opener won't get over-enthusiastic or expect that a slam must be available.

Exchanging the two red suits would mean that, in order to give a positive response showing diamonds, you would have to bid 3◊ because, as you will remember, 2◊ is the negative. You really are not good enough to raise the bidding to this level, so it would be wiser to bid the negative 2◊ in the first place, and then to take any opportunity of encouraging, to show that, even if negative, your hand is not worthless.

(Bids: 2♡ and 2◊)

26 ♠ Q 9 7   Your partner deals and opens 2♣.
   ♡ K 9 8   What would you respond and
   ◇ Q J 6   would it make any difference if
   ♣ K J 8 7   your black suits were exchanged?

Answer: With the hand as it is, containing 12 points and no really biddable suit, you are much too good for a negative response of 2◇. You could, of course, make a positive response of 3♣, but this uses a good deal of bidding space simply for the sake of mentioning a suit in which you are not really anxious to play. Bid a positive 2NT, and await developments.

A four-card major suit is always biddable so, if your clubs and spades were exchanged, it would be more economical in bidding space to make your positive response 2♠ rather than 2NT. In other words, if you can show a biddable suit without raising the level of the bidding, do so, but bear in mind that, in practice, it is wiser to conceal even a four-card major unless it is headed by at least the K–J.

(Bids: 2NT and 2♠)

27 ♠ K J 9   Your partner deals and opens with
   ♡ A K Q 10   a pre-emptive 3♠. What, if any-
   ◇ A Q J 9 6   thing, would you respond?
   ♣ 9

Answer: Unfortunately sometimes, when partner has a hand on which he wants to make a pre-emptive bid, it is responder who is in trouble, when he himself has a very powerful hand. However, there are guiding principles to help.

Just as a change-of-suit at the one-level is a one-round force, so a change-of-suit at this high level is also a one-round force, provided it is a bid below game level. In principle a major suit bid, if not already at game level (as 3♡–3♠), is a game try, and a minor-suit bid is a slam try agreeing opener's suit as trumps.

In this case, therefore, responder should bid 4◇, not because he wants to play in this suit but because he is perfectly willing to play in spades. Opener should now show any other feature his hand may contain, but the least he will do is rebid his suit.

(Bid: 4◇)

28 ♠ 8 2   Your partner deals and opens with
   ♡ K J 10 9 5 4 3   a pre-emptive 3♠. What would
   ◇ 7 2   you respond?
   ♣ A K

Answer: The most elementary rule for responding to partner's
pre-emptive opening is never to rescue into a suit which you
have absolutely no guarantee will make a safer contract than his.
There's just one thing to do here, and that's to pass – partner's
spades may even be better than your hearts, and in addition to
side-suit values, you have a doubleton spade for him.

Exchange your major suits, giving yourself long spades and let
partner open 3♡, and you would still pass. Remember that 3♠
would be a one-round force, so the contract would have to climb
to the four-level. If you had a long and solid suit in addition to
your ♣A–K, it would be only sensible to bid it at game level,
which your partner could hardly misunderstand.

(Bid: No Bid)

29 ♠ 9 3   Your partner deals and opens 5♠.
   ♡ 4 3   What would you respond?
   ◇ A K 6
   ♣ A K J 9 6 4

Answer: By using this conventional opening bid, your partner is
saying that nothing is any use to him except either the ace or king
of his trump suit. If he has made the correct opening bid, which
you must, of course, assume, you can expect him to have very
long spades headed by the ♠Q–J–10, top hearts, and voids in
both minors, so your diamond and club honours will be useless.

With either the ace or king of spades, even if singleton, you
would raise to 6♠ and with both you would raise to 7♠. With
neither you pass, which is only answering the question you have
been asked.

(Bid: No Bid)

30 ♠ K Q J 9 7 4   Your partner deals and opens 4NT.
   ♡ A 7 4 3   What would you respond?
   ◇ 9 6
   ♣ 8

Answer: 4NT is another conventional opening bid which requires *only* the answer to the question you have been asked – have you any ace at all, and if so, which? Doubtless opener has a hand on which he fears that if he finally enquires about your ace-holding via a Blackwood 4NT, he may find it difficult to know whether a 5 ◊ one-ace response shows the ace he vitally needs or a worthless one.

In response to a 4NT opening you must ignore anything in your hand other than aces. With no ace bid 5♣. With one ace, cue-bid it, that is, with the ◊ A, ♡ A, or ♠ A, bid five of that suit or, with the ♣ A, bid 6♣. With two aces, bid 5NT. So here you cue-bid your ♡ A.

(Bid: 5♡)

Competition quiz

In competition against another player, one should answer the three questions in the **A** set, and the other the three questions in the **B** set on each page.

1A Your partner deals and opens 1♡. What would you respond?

1	♠ A J 9 4	2	♠ 9	3	♠ J 8 6
	♡ J 8 6		♡ Q 8 6		♡ A J 9 4
	◊ 7 5 4		◊ A 9 7 6 4		◊ J 10 2
	♣ J 10 2		♣ 9 8 6 5		♣ 7 5 4

Answers:

Bid	Reason
(2 points)	(3 points)

1 1♠ This change-of-suit promises no more than 1NT would do.

2 2♡ A single raise of partner's suit normally promises four-card trump support, but 2♡ is more realistic than 1NT or 2◊.

3 2♡ This is a genuine limit-bid, between 6–9 points and four-card trump support.

1B Your partner deals and opens 1♡. What would you respond?

1 ♠ Q 9 5	2 ♠ Q 9	3 ♠ Q 9 5
♡ Q 9 7	♡ J 9 7 2	♡ Q 9 7
◊ K Q 8 7 4	◊ K Q 8 7 4	◊ J 10 8 7 4
♣ Q 8	♣ 9 8	♣ Q 8

Answers:

Bid		Reason
(2 points)		(3 points)
1	2◊	Lacking four-card heart support, you have the necessary minimum of 8 points for a change-of-suit response at the two-level.
2	2♡	A normal limit-bid on 6–9 points and four-card trump support. Don't change the suit to 2◊ when you needn't.
3	1NT	You lack four-card trump support but, with at least a doubleton honour in each suit, there is no need to bend the rule by raising hearts. Bid 1NT.

2A Your partner deals and opens 1♣. What would you respond?

1 ♠ 9 8 6 3	2 ♠ 9 8 6	3 ♠ 9 8 6
♡ K 7 4	♡ K 7 4	♡ K J 4 3
◊ Q J 5	◊ Q J 5	◊ Q J 5
♣ J 9 7	♣ Q J 9 7	♣ Q J 7

Answers:

Bid		Reason
(2 points)		(3 points)
1	1♠	Your hand is not strong enough for a response of 1NT, which shows 8–10 points when facing a 1♣ opening. 1♠ at this stage only confirms that you have a little something.
2	1NT	This count-showing response is likely to be far more constructive than a raise in clubs. Opener will know you have between 8–10 points and, automatically, some fit for clubs.
3	1♡	Even though you have 10 points on which you could

respond 1NT, you have a biddable heart suit which might be useful. As the bid is a one-round force you are sure of a chance to bid again if it seems expedient.

2B Your partner deals and opens 1♦. What would you respond?

1 ♠ J 8 6 3	2 ♠ 9 8 6	3 ♠ 9 8 6
♡ K 7 4	♡ K 7 4	♡ K 7 4
♦ Q J 5	♦ Q J 5 3	♦ Q J 5
♣ J 10 7	♣ J 10 7	♣ J 10 7 3

Answers:

Bid	Reason
(2 points)	(3 points)

1   1♠   You have, in fact, a choice between 1♠ and 1NT, but 1♠ is the better.

2   2♦   Again you have a choice, 1NT or 2♦, but the latter is the better, as you have at least got four-card diamond support, and no stop in spades this time.

3   1NT   Even without any stop in spades your only sensible bid is 1NT, which shows your 6–9 points, as well as keeping the bidding open in case partner is strong.

3A Your partner deals and opens 1♠. What would you respond?

1 ♠ Q 10 9	2 ♠ Q 9 7 2	3 ♠ 8 6 5 4
♡ Q J 4	♡ Q J 7	♡ K 6
♦ A 9 7 2	♦ A 9 7	♦ A K 9 5 4
♣ Q 10 6	♣ Q 10 6	♣ 6 3

Answers:

Bid	Reason
(2 points)	(3 points)

1   2NT   This is another of the Acol limit-bids and though not forcing, is encouraging. It shows 10–12 points on an evenly-balanced hand, and denies four-card support for partner's major suit opening.

2   3♠   Here you have four-card spade support and the

necessary 10–12 points. A non-forcing but encouraging limit-bid, raising the auction to a dangerously high level if your left-hand opponent wants to come in.

3   3♠   This limit-bid, guaranteeing four-card trump support, is far better Acol technique than a change-of-suit to 2◊. Announce your full strength in one bid, promising 10–12 points and four-card trump support. Don't be tempted to bid your diamonds.

3B   Your partner deals and opens 1◊. What would you respond?

1 ♠ 9 8 7 5	2 ♠ A 7 2	3 ♠ Q 7
♡ A Q J 6 2	♡ 10 6 5	♡ 10 9 6
◊ K 3	◊ K J 6 2	◊ Q 8 4
♣ 9 3	♣ K 9 2	♣ A Q J 6 2

Answers:

Bid		Reason
(2 points)		(3 points)
1	1♡	A perfectly normal change-of-suit response showing a biddable suit. You choose your longest suit, hearts.
2	3◊	With the values for a limit-bid at the three-level and no more constructive bid available, this is your best choice. If partner takes out into 3NT, which your strong raise invites, pass happily.
3	2♣	Quite unsuitable for a bid in no-trumps at this stage and also not fitted for a diamond raise. You have the strength for a change-of-suit at the two-level.

4A   Your partner deals and opens 1♡. What would you respond and would it make any difference if you had dealt and passed originally?

1 ♠ 9 3	2 ♠ 9 7 5	3 ♠ 8 5 3
♡ J 9 8 6 2	♡ 10 9	♡ K 9 7 2
◊ 6	◊ A Q J 6 4	◊ 4
♣ K Q J 6 4	♣ K 6 5	♣ K Q J 8 2

Answers:

Bids   Reasons
(1 point each)   (1½ points each)

1   4♡   A pre-emptive attempt to keep your left-hand oppo-
          nent out of the auction.
     3♡   As you know your left hand opponent could not open,
          he is hardly likely to be able to come in over 3♡.
2   2◊   A simple change-of-suit response for which you have
          the values.
     2◊   Exactly the same – you only just failed to open!
3   3♡   Full values for the straight limit-bid. Position at the
     3♡   table or interference by your opponents makes no
          difference.

4B Your partner deals and opens 1◊. What would you
respond and would it make any difference if you had dealt
and passed originally?

    1 ♠ J 10 4   2 ♠ J 10 4   3 ♠ K 9 2
       ♡ A 10 7   ♡ A 10 7 4   ♡ Q 7 4
       ◊ J 8 7 6   ◊ J 8 7 6   ◊ J 8 7 6
       ♣ 6 3 2   ♣ 6 2   ♣ A Q 6

Answers:

Bids   Reasons
(1 point each)   (1½ points each)

1   2◊   This is the only sensible response in either situation.
     2◊   The fact that you have already passed makes no
          difference.
2   1♡   This may prove to be the most constructive response
          and you will always have a chance to put opener back
          into diamonds.
     2◊   Once having passed, 1♡ would not be forcing, and
          there is a risk of being left in this contract when the
          hand 'belongs' in diamonds.
3   2NT The 11–12 point limit-bid in either case. Your only
     2NT alternative is 3◊, but it is more likely to encourage
          partner into a 3NT contract to show your evenly-
          balanced shape rather than raise diamonds.

5A Your partner deals and opens 1♡. What would you respond?

1 ♠ 8	2 ♠ A K Q J 9 5 4	3 ♠ K Q 10 6 4
♡ K Q 10 6	♡ 7	♡ 8
◊ K Q 9 4 3	◊ A 6	◊ K Q 9 3
♣ A K 7	♣ 6 3 2	♣ A K 7

Answers:

Bid		Reason
(2 points)		(3 points)

1   3♣ Knowing that the hand will play eventually in hearts, make a forcing bid of 3♣ (choosing the suit in which you have the best 'tops'). This announces 'game certain, slam possible'.

2   2♠ If you don't make a forcing bid immediately you may find yourself in difficulties on the next round.

3   1♠ The same honour count as 1 but with the complete lack of fit for partner's bid suit it is better to make a simple one-round force and await developments. You can always make a forcing rebid.

5B Your partner deals and opens 1♡. What would you respond?

1 ♠ A Q J 9 3	2 ♠ K J 2	3 ♠ K Q 5
♡ K J 6	♡ 6	♡ Q 3
◊ K J 5 2	◊ A K 10 9 5	◊ A K J 9 5
♣ 9	♣ K Q 7 4	♣ J 10 7

Answers:

Bid		Reason
(2 points)		(3 points)

1   2♠ Another hand where an immediate force is mandatory. A game is as near certain as anything could be, and a slam is quite probable, particularly if opener has diamond tops for you.

2   2◊ The complete lack of a heart fit makes it wiser to go slowly here. You can always force on the next round if expedient.

3   3◊ The ♡Q–x is by no means a misfit and the force, after

all, only commits you to a game, not necessarily to an astronomical contract.

6A Your partner deals and opens 1♡. What would you respond?

1 ♠ K J 6	2 ♠ A J 7	3 ♠ K 9 6
♡ K 10 7 6	♡ K J 7 6	♡ K 10 8 3
◇ A Q J 8	◇ A Q J 8	◇ A J 9 8
♣ 9 3	♣ J 10	♣ 9 3

Answers:

Bid	Reason
(2 points)	(3 points)

1   2◇   This hand is too strong for a limit-bid of 3♡ which might be passed, and it's not quite strong enough for a forcing response. The way to deal with it is via a delayed game raise, 2◇ on the first round and a jump to game next.

2   3◇   Too strong for either a limit-bid or the delayed game raise technique. Make an immediate game force, choosing the suit ranking below the bid suit in which you have 'tops'.

3   3♡   A straightforward limit-bid showing 10–12 points and four-card heart support.

6B Your partner deals and opens 1♠. What would you respond?

1 ♠ J 10 8 7	2 ♠ K J 6 2	3 ♠ K J 6 2
♡ –	♡ J 7 4	♡ J 7 4
◇ A K J 9	◇ A J 7 2	◇ 8 5
♣ K Q 10 7 4	♣ 8 5	♣ A K Q 6

Answers:

Bid	Reason
(2 points)	(3 points)

1   3♣   Too strong for anything other than an immediate force. Note that you choose the suit in which you have the A–K rather than the longer clubs. You are fully prepared to play in spades and you will find that

partner will expect first round control of the suit in which you force.

2   3♠   The straightforward limit-bid again, with ten honour points and one distributional point (the doubleton club).

3   2♣   Too strong for a limit-bid and not quite strong enough to force. Respond 2♣ intending to raise to 4♠ if opener rebids 2◇, 2♡ or 2♠.

7A   Your partner deals and opens 1♡. What would you respond?

1 ♠ A 9 3 2	2 ♠ A 9 3 2	3 ♠ A 9 3
♡ K Q 8 4	♡ K 9 8 4	♡ A J 8 4
◇ A 10 6 4	◇ K J 10 6	◇ A 10 6 4
♣ 3 2	♣ 3	♣ 3 2

Answers:

Bid		Reason
(2 points)		(3 points)

1   4♣   This is a Swiss conventional response. There are several versions of this convention but one excellent one uses a response of 4♣ to show four-card trump support, two aces, and 13–15 points. The hand is too good for a limit-bid of 3♡ and not good enough for an immediate force.

2   1♠   The same count as 1 but lacking the specific requirement of two aces. Too strong for a 3♡ limit-bid, so use the delayed game raise technique.

3   4◇   A Swiss conventional bid, again showing four-card trump support and three aces in a 13–15 point hand.

7B   Your partner deals and opens 1♠. What would you respond?

1 ♠ K J 8 3	2 ♠ K J 8	3 ♠ A 9 3 2
♡ A 10 6 4	♡ A 10 6	♡ A 10 7 4
◇ 8	◇ A J 8 3 2	◇ 8
♣ J 10 9 3	♣ 3 2	♣ K J 6 2

Answers:

Bid		Reason
(2 points)		(3 points)

1 3♠ Counting 2 points for the singleton diamond, this is a perfect hand for this strong limit-bid.

2 2◇ Although you have two aces and good trump support, you can't make a spade limit-bid or a Swiss bid at this stage. If partner *re*bids spades over your 2◇, you can put him to 4♠, as then you will know he has at least a five-card suit.

3 4♣ The Swiss response showing four-card trump support, two aces, and 13–15 points with insufficient strength to make a forcing take-out, though being unwilling to play below game-level.

8A Your partner deals and opens 1♠. What would you respond?

1 ♠ K 10 8 4	2 ♠ K 10 8 4	3 ♠ K 10 8 4
♡ K 9 3	♡ A 9 3	♡ A 9 3
◇ Q 4	◇ Q 4	◇ A Q
♣ 9 8 4 2	♣ K Q 9 8	♣ 9 8 4 2

Answers:

Bid		Reason
(2 points)		(3 points)

1 2♠ The simple limit-bid confirming four-card trump support and the inability to make any stronger bid.

2 2♣ Too strong for a limit-bid which might be passed out, not strong enough for a force, and an immediate 4♠ might cost a missed slam. A delayed game raise starting with a 2♣ change-of-suit is indicated.

3 4♣ The Swiss bid showing the trump fit, two aces, and 13–15 points.

8B Your partner deals and opens 1♠. What would you respond?

1 ♠ K Q 8 4	2 ♠ J 10 8 7 6	3 ♠ K 10 8 4
♡ A 9 3	♡ 5 4	♡ A 9 3
◇ A K	◇ K Q J 6 2	◇ Q J
♣ 9 8 4 2	♣ 5	♣ 9 8 4 2

Answers:

Bid   Reason
(2 points)   (3 points)

1   3◇   Much too strong for anything but an immediate game
            force proclaiming 'game certain, slam possible'.

2   4♠   This is not a limit-bid intended to encourage partner
            to explore for a slam. It says that you think there
            should be a play for game on your 'shape' and that
            you want to try to pre-empt your left-hand opponent
            out of the auction.

3   3♠   A straightforward encouraging limit-bid showing
            four-card trump support and 10–12 high card and
            distributional points.

9A   Your partner deals and opens 2♡. What would you
     respond?

     1 ♠ K 9 8 4 2   2 ♠ K 9 8 4 2   3 ♠ Q 9 8 4 2
        ♡ 7 6   ♡ A 7 2   ♡ K 7 2
        ◇ A 9 3   ◇ 7 6 4   ◇ 7 6 4
        ♣ 8 4 2   ♣ 9 7   ♣ 8 4 2

Answers:

Bid   Reason
(2 points)   (3 points)

1   2♠   Just worth a positive response as this can be given
            without raising the level of the auction.

2   3♡   Any positive response to a strong two makes the
            sequence forcing to game, but it is better to confirm
            partner's suit as trumps at once, far more likely to
            interest him than 2♠.

3   2NT   Insufficient values for a positive response, even
            though there is a biddable spade suit. If opener rebids
            3♡, raise to 4♡.

9B   Your partner deals and opens 2♠. What would you
     respond?

     1 ♠ K 9 7 2   2 ♠ J 9   3 ♠ K J 9
        ♡ K 6 4   ♡ K 9 7 2   ♡ K Q 7 6 2
        ◇ Q 9 3 2   ◇ K 9 8   ◇ A 6 2
        ♣ K 7   ♣ Q J 8 4   ♣ 8 4

Answers:

Bid	Reason
(2 points)	(3 points)

1   4♠   The immediate double raise shows good trump support, 10–12 points, but *no* ace or void.

2   3NT   The approximate equivalent of a limit-bid of 2NT points facing a one-level opening, though facing a strong two it denies a biddable suit and, by inference, denies a trump fit good enough for a raise to the four-level.

3   3♠   The spade support is more than adequate for a suit good enough to open at the two-level. The single raise, besides agreeing the trump suit, also promises at least one ace or void.

10A Your partner deals and opens 2♡. What would you respond?

1 ♠ 9 7	2 ♠ 9 7 4	3 ♠ –
♡ –	♡ 10 3	♡ K 9 7 4
◇ A K Q J 10 8 7 5	◇ 8 4	◇ K 7 5 3
♣ 9 6 4	♣ K Q 9 8 6 4	♣ K J 8 6 3

Answers:

Bid	Reason
(2 points)	(3 points)

1   4◇   This is a jump bid in a forcing situation (as 2♡ is a one-round force). It shows a solid self-supporting trump suit for which no fit or support is needed.

2   2NT   Though the clubs would just be worth showing if this could be done without raising the bidding level, a positive response would make the sequence forcing to game.

3   3♡   A single raise promises a good trump fit and at least one first-round control – in this case the spade void.

10B Your partner deals and opens 2♠. What would you respond?

1 ♠ 9 7	2 ♠ 9 3	3 ♠ Q J 9 7
♡ K 10 8 4	♡ 8 7	♡ A K Q J 10 9 3
◇ A 7 6	◇ K Q J 10 8 6 5	◇ 8
♣ 9 8 7 5	♣ K 9	♣ 7

Answers:

Bid		Reason
(2 points)		(3 points)

1   2NT   Even with an ace and king it is better to give a negative response on the first round. You can't support spades or bid a red suit, and 3NT would deny an ace. (A 2♡ opening you would, of course, have raised to 3♡.)

2   3◇   A natural bid in your own good suit which by inference denies ability to support partner's suit.

3   4NT   With this superb spade fit all you need to know for a slam is whether you are missing one or two aces. If partner has only one (unlikely) you can stop in 5♠.

11A Your partner deals and opens 3♡. What would you respond?

1 ♠ A K J 6	2 ♠ A K Q J 7 6	3 ♠ K J 10 9 7 6 4
♡ K Q 3	♡ 5	♡ 8
◇ A Q J 6 2	◇ K Q J 10	◇ 9 5
♣ 7	♣ 10 7	♣ A Q 4

Answers:

Bid		Reason
(2 points)		(3 points)

1   4◇   A change-of-suit response to an opening pre-emptive bid, if it is one below game level, is a one-round force. In principle a minor suit response should be taken as a slam invitation in the suit opened and a major suit response as a game invitation which may be raised on as good as Q–x in support.

2   4♠   Not being slam-minded the best bid is an immediate 4♠ which opener can hardly misunderstand.

3   No   Never 'rescue' into a suit which you have no assur-
     Bid   ance will be better than partner's. The thing he's *least* likely to hold is good spade support!

11B Your partner deals and opens 3♡. What would you respond?

1 ♠ A 10 7	2 ♠ 9	3 ♠ A Q 10 7 6
♡ J 9 4	♡ Q 9 8 6 2	♡ K 10 7
◇ A Q 6	◇ Q 8 4	◇ 8
♣ K Q 10 9	♣ J 7 5 3	♣ A Q 7 3

Answers:

Bid		Reason
(2 points)		(3 points)
1	4♡	Even facing a weak three you must have at least a play for game with 3½ honour tricks. Raise partner to 4♡.
2	4♡	This is not because you have a hope of making it but to make it as difficult as possible for your left-hand opponent to come into the auction. Partner's weak three plus your 5 points won't go far in defence!
3	4♡	Not quite the power to be slam-minded and not much point in suggesting a spade game contract with such excellent support for hearts. Reverse your heart and diamond holdings, though, and you should bid 3♠.

12A Your partner deals and opens 2♣. What would you respond?

1 ♠ Q 10 8 7 4	2 ♠ Q 10 8 7 4	3 ♠ 9 3
♡ A 6 2	♡ 7 6 2	♡ A K Q J 10 8 5
◇ K J 4	◇ K 9 3	◇ 7 2
♣ 8 3	♣ 8 3	♣ 8 5

Answers:

Bid		Reason
(2 points)		(3 points)
1	2♠	A positive response showing your biddable suit in a hand which contains not only the requirement of one ace and one king, but the other of any 8 points.
2	2◇	A negative response denying the values to make any constructive bid at this stage.
3	3♡	A forcing situation is in being here, so the jump bid shows a solid and self-supporting trump suit. Even if

partner has a heart void you can play in a heart slam without any misgivings.

12B Your partner deals and opens 2♣. What would you respond?

	1 ♠ K 10 8	2 ♠ K J 8	3 ♠ A 10
	♡ J 9 7 4	♡ 7 6 2	♡ K J 9 4
	◇ Q J 6	◇ A 10 9 6 5	◇ Q J 6 3
	♣ K 7 2	♣ 8 3	♣ 7 6 2

Answers:

Bid		Reason
(2 points)		(3 points)
1	2NT	A positive response showing at least 8 honour points and no biddable suit.
2	3◇	As 2◇ would be the negative response, it is necessary to show positive values with a biddable diamond suit by going to 3◇ which is not, of course, a jump bid in any other sense of the word.
3	2♡	This is a perfectly biddable suit in a hand with good – extremely good – positive values. You would willingly bid it as the one-level, and can do so now.

Section 3

No-trump Bidding

The basic rules

Examples of no-trump opening bids, both weak and strong, were given in Section 1, so here we concern ourselves with responding and to the possible development of the subsequent auction.

The strength of an opening no-trump is a matter of partnership agreement, and from then onwards, many of the responses are a question of simple arithmetic, based on the table below. These counts are, of course, arbitrary, and as your experience develops you will learn to give due weight to suit length, the quality of controls and intermediates, and so on. Note too that the minimum of 25 points shown as necessary for a game in no-trumps is very conservative, and many a successful game can be made on less, particularly as declarer-skill develops.

No-trump contracts

25–26 points between two evenly-balanced hands for a game.
33–34 points between two evenly-balanced hands for a small slam.
37 points between two evenly-balanced hands for a grand slam.

Suit contracts

26 points with a trump fit for a major suit game.
28–29 points with a trump fit for a minor suit game.
31–33 points with a trump fit for a small slam.
37 points with a trump fit for a grand slam.

1 *Direct raises of no-trump openings:*

1NT weak (12–14 points)	Raise to 2NT on 11 or a poor quality 12 points, invitational but *not* forcing. Raise direct to 3NT on 13 points.
1NT strong (15–17 points)	Raise to 2NT on 8–9 points, invitational but not forcing. Raise direct to 3NT on 10 points.
2NT (20–22 points)	Raise to 3NT on 5 points, or 4 points in a five-card suit.
1NT weak 1NT strong 2NT	Raise to 4NT quantitatively and invitationally if the combined minimum count is 31 points. Raise to 6NT if the combined minimum count is 33–34 points and cannot reach 37 points. Raise direct to 7NT if the combined minimum count is 37 or more points. Raise to 5NT if the combined minimum count is 35 points and a maximum count in the opening hand may bring it to the grand slam requirements of 37 points. This opening demands a rebid of 6NT on a minimum hand and 7NT on a maximum.

2 *Suit take-out of no-trump opening:*

The values needed depend on the known strength of the opening no-trump, as a hand worth only a weak take-out facing 12–14 points may be worth a game facing 15–17 points. Whatever the strength of the opening bid:

2◇, 2♡, 2♠	Shows a weak unbalanced hand better fitted for a suit contract – a five-card or longer suit and no game ambitions.
3♡, 3♠	A game force showing the values to play in game, either suit or no-trumps.
3♣, 3◇	Slam invitation in the minor.

4♡, 4♠, 5♣, 5♢	Pre-emptive shut-out bids based on very unbalanced hands with at least a seven-card suit.
2♣	Conventional fit-finding bid of unrevealed strength showing interest in a major suit contract.
4♣	Conventional Gerber request to show aces. In response, 4♢ = no ace or four; 4♡ = one ace; 4♠ = two aces; 4NT = three aces. A 5♣ rebid then asks for kings on the same 'step' scale.

3 *2♣ Response to* 1NT – *opener's rebids and responder's actions:*

2♢	Rebid by opener, denies a four-card major holding, irrespective of opener's diamonds or his point count.
1NT–2♣ 2♢–2♡	Responder may now, according to strength, make a weak take-out, or even pass 2♢ if that seems wisest. Alternatively responder may convert to
1NT–2♣ 2♢–3♣	2NT or 3NT according to his values. He may also repeat clubs at the three-level, which shows a long weak club suit, and no interest in a game contract.
1NT–2♣ 2♢–3♠	A jump rebid by responder is now highly invitational but not forcing, showing a hand on which he is doubtful about going on to game once a four-card fit for his major suit is known to be missing.
1NT–2♣ 2♢–3♢	Responder's 3♢ rebid asks for opener's *better* major. Opener should show the longer of the two and, if both are of equal length, the stronger.
1NT–2♣ 2♡	In response to the 2♣ bid, opener should show a four-card major suit if held. With both he should bid hearts first. Responder may now, according to
1NT–2♣ 2♠–3♠ or 4♠ or 2NT or 3NT	his strength and whether or not the hoped-for-fit has been discovered, pass the two-level bid, raise invitationally to the three-level, raise direct to the suit game, or convert to 2 or 3NT. Responder must never bid 2♣ in the first place unless, whatever opener replies, he himself has a rebid available.

1NT–2♣	SID convention agreeing major suit fit but offering
2♡–3◇	opener choice of 3NT or 4 of a major contract.
	(Stayman In Doubt.) No ruffing values.

4 *Suit take-out of* 2NT *opening and opener's rebids:*

2NT—3♡	Forcing to game and a mild slam try on a hand
or 3♠	which must be played in the suit named. Opener's
	rebid of 4NT would be conventional.

| 2NT–4♡ | At least four points with a long suit. A sign-off, |
| or 4♠ | which opener should pass. |

| 2NT–3♣ | Requests opener to show four-card suits in ascending order and, if his only four-card suit is clubs, to rebid 3NT. (The Baron convention.) |

| 2NT–3◇ | Flint request to opener to transfer to 3♡ which |
| 3♡ | responder can either pass (weak take-out) or 'correct' to 3♠ if that is his long weak suit. |

2NT–3◇	Opener can occasionally elect to force a game
3♠ or	contract with a *maximum* hand. With a very strong
3NT	heart fit, he rebids 3♠ which responder can pass or convert to hearts at the four-level or, with a strong fit for both majors, opener can force responder to select his suit at the four-level by bidding 3NT.

| 2NT–3◇ | Responder can show a genuine diamond suit and |
| 3♡–3NT | mild slam ambitions by taking out opener's forced response into 3NT. |

| 2NT–4♣ | Gerber, as over 1NT. |

Note: Exactly the same sequences are used when the bidding has started 2♣–2◇–2NT, except that responder must allow for the greater announced strength of his partner's opening bid (23–24 points).

5 *Other no-trumps openings:*

| 3NT | This is a tactical bid based on a long solid minor suit. Pass unless you have something obviously |

better to bid. It is not an opening bid to concern learners who would do better to open suitable hands with a pre-emptive bid in the minor suit concerned.

4NT   A conventional opening bid requiring responder to show aces immediately on the following scale:

With no ace, 5♣; with the ♣A, 6♣; with the ◇A, ♡A, or ♠A, five of the suit in which the ace is held; with two aces, 5NT.

Exercises

1   ♠ J 9 5   Your partner deals and opens 1NT.
     ♡ Q 4   What would you respond if the
     ◇ Q 8 7 3   agreed strength were 12–14 points,
     ♣ K J 7 4   and what if it were 15–17 points?

Answer: On evenly-balanced hands when no question of taking out into a suit arises, the only point for responder to consider is the combined strength of the two hands. If this reaches 25–26 points he should raise direct to 3NT.

If he is doubtful, that is, if opener needs to have his maximum rather than his minimum for game values, then responder should raise invitationally to 2NT.

Here, with 9 points to add to opener's known maximum of 14 points it is impossible for game values to be held and responder should pass. If, on the other hand, the known opening values held were 15–17 points, this becomes a joint minimum of 24 points, and responder should raise invitationally to 2NT.

Many an expert player is happy to be in 3NT on a combined 24 points, but as learners you would do well to work on the higher count.

(Bids: No Bid and 2NT)

2 ♠ A Q 7 4   Your partner deals and opens 1NT.
   ♡ J 9 5   What would you respond if the
   ◇ Q 8 6   agreed strength were 12–14 points,
   ♣ Q 7 2   and what if it were 15–17 points?

Answer: This is another exercise in simple arithmetic. Facing a known minimum of 12 points responder can see a certain 23 points between the combined hands but to reach game values opener must hold his maximum of 14 points, or at any rate a 'good quality' 13 points, so responder should raise invitationally to 2NT.

Facing a 15–17 point no-trump responder knows that the combined minimum is 26 points, so he should raise direct to 3NT. He must not leave the onus on opener by bidding only 2NT, as opener, with his minimum of 15 points, would pass.

(Bids: 2NT and 3NT)

3 ♠ Q 8 3   Your partner deals and opens 1NT.
   ♡ A Q 9   What would you respond if the
   ◇ A 7 4   agreed strength were 12–14 points,
   ♣ J 6 5 3   and what if it were 15–17 points?

Answer: With 13 points facing a minimum of 12 points there is no need to look further than an immediate raise to 3NT. The combined count cannot be less than 25 points, nor more than 27 points, not up to slam requirements but comfortably at the game level.

When the combined count is a good deal higher than game requirements, responder must next make sure it isn't up to the slam level. Even facing the maximum of 17 points in a strong no-trump, the combined total cannot be more than 30 points, insufficient on which to bid a slam. Again, responder should simply bid 3NT.

(Bids: 3NT in either case)

4 ♠ K J 7   Your partner deals and opens 1NT.
   ♡ A Q 7   What would you respond if the
   ◇ K 9 8 4   agreed strength were 12–14 points,
   ♣ A Q 3   and what if it were 15–17 points?

Answer: 19 points facing a minimum of 12 add up to 31, below the requirements for a slam on two evenly-balanced hands. But if partner has 14 . . . .? Bid a quantitative, *not* conventional 4NT, which your partner will understand as an invitation to go to 6NT if his hand is maximum strength. With a minimum he will pass.

Facing a 15–17 point no-trump, the combined minimum must be 34 points, within the 33–35 point range, which makes a small slam contract a good proposition, so the only other question is whether a grand slam should be bid. For this there should be a minimum of 37 points between the two hands, and your 19 points added to your partner's maximum of 17 points, cannot be more than 36 points. So here responder should just bid 6NT with no beating about the bush.

(Bids: 4NT and 6NT)

5 ♠ A 7   Your partner deals and opens 1NT.
   ♡ K J 8 7 5 4   What would you respond if the
   ◊ 9 5   agreed strength were 12–14 points,
   ♣ J 7 2   and what if it were 15–17 points?

Answer: Facing a maximum of 14 points, you would need to find every adverse card lying 'right' to make a game, and it is also obvious that the hand should be played in hearts, not in no-trumps. Bid 2♡, a weak take-out, which opener is expected to pass.

Facing a strong no-trump, which contains a known minimum of 15 points, you want to be in a game contract but would prefer hearts to no-trumps. Bid 3♡, a forcing-to-game bid, and opener will either convert to 3NT or raise to 4♡. He has one other possibility, which you will meet in hand 8.

(Bids: 2♡ and 3♡)

6 ♠ 10 9 7 5 3 2   Your partner deals and opens 1NT.
   ♡ 9 6 2   What would you respond if the
   ◊ J 10 3   agreed strength were 12–14 points,
   ♣ 7   and what if it were 15–17 points?

Answer: It makes no difference whether partner's opening no-trump is weak or strong – this hand won't run to a game contract, and it isn't even likely to produce a plus score unless it can be played in spades. In either case, therefore, take out into 2♠.

Many players still have the idea that a weak take-out is for use facing a weak no-trump only. This is quite incorrect, as it doesn't matter whether the opening hand is weak or strong as long as responder is sure of two things, first that the combined hands won't produce a game and second, that they are likely to play better in a suit than in no-trumps. Note also that weak take-out bids can be made in spades, hearts, and diamonds, but not in clubs which, as you will see in later examples, is used conventionally.

(Bids: 2♠ in either case)

7	♠ A 9 6 4	Being not vulnerable you open
	♡ J 10	1NT as dealer. What would you
	◊ K J 6 2	rebid if partner responds:
	♣ K 7 4	(a) 2♡ (b) 2NT (c) 3♠ (d) 3♡?

Answers:

(a) Partner's 2♡ is a weak take-out, and even though it has come in your own poorest suit you must respect his decision and pass.

(b) 2NT is invitational, an invitation which, on your minimum hand, you reserve your right to refuse. Pass.

(c) 3♠ is game-forcing, leaving you to choose between 3NT and 4♠. With this excellent spade fit the latter is the correct choice.

(d) 3♡ is also game-forcing, but warn your partner of your poor, no better than a doubleton, fit by rebidding 3NT. Don't panic if he removes to 4♡.

(Bids: No Bid, No Bid, 4♠ and 3NT)

8	♠ K 8 7	Again not vulnerable, you open
	♡ Q 10 6 3	1NT. What would you rebid if
	◊ K J 9	partner responds:
	♣ A J 7	(a) 2◊ (b) 2NT (c) 3♡?

Answers:

(a) Even with your maximum of 14 points you must respect partner's decision and pass.

(b) 2NT is, as you know, invitational, and this time you have no hesitation in accepting the invitation to go on to 3NT.

(c) Here we meet a new situation. Responder has made a game force, at the same time saying that he fancies a heart contract. You have a maximum for your bid – in fact ½ a point over – and, too, your best suit is hearts. In such circumstances, when you would in any case raise to 4♡, make an advance cue-bid of 4♣ on the way. This shows trump agreement, a maximum opening no-trump, and the ace of the cue-bid suit.

(Bids: No Bid, 3NT and 4♣)

9 ♠ 10 9 8 5 4   Your partner deals and opens 1NT.
  ♡ J 9 6 5 3   What would you respond if the
  ◇ J 8   strength were 12–14 points, and
  ♣ 7   what if it were 15–17 points?

Answer: Clearly this hand won't run to a game contract whether opener is strong, let alone only holding 12–14 points, so whichever you know he has, you would cope in the same way. You would prefer to play in spades or hearts, but who are you to guess which will fit his hand better? *Ask* by bidding a conventional Stayman 2♣.

2♣ is a request to opener to show any major four-card holding. With both he should bid the hearts first and with neither he should rebid 2◇ irrespective of his actual diamond holding. Responder can now judge whether to pass at the two-level, raise the suit invitationally to the three-level, bid a suit game contract direct or, if the response is not what he wanted to hear, convert to 2 or 3NT, according to strength. The one essential for responder is that, before he bids 2♣, he should make sure he has a sensible course of action he can take on the next round. Here he would pass a 2♡ or 2♠ rebid, or convert 2◇ to 2♡, his slightly better suit.

(Bids: 2♣ in either case)

10 ♠ Q 9 7 4   Your partner deals and opens 1NT.
  ♡ K 6 3 2   What would you respond if the
  ◇ 10   strength were 12–14 points, and
  ♣ Q J 4 2   what if it were 15–17 points?

Answer: Here's a case in point where, facing a 12–14 point no-trump, there is nothing sensible you can do on the next round if, in reply to 2♣ from you, partner rebids 2◊. Your two major suits are neither good enough to 'rescue' yourself into one of them at the two-level, and you haven't enough points to convert to 2NT which would tell partner you could have bid 2NT in the first place. All you can do, therefore, is to pass.

Facing a strong no-trump you *could* raise 1NT to 2NT invitationally, so you can take your chance to bid 2♣ to ask partner if he has four spades or hearts. If he says yes, you can raise invitationally to three of the suit, and if he says no by bidding 2◊ you can convert to 2NT.

(Bids: No Bid and 2♣)

11 ♠ K Q 9 8
    ♡ A Q 7 4 3
    ◊ 9
    ♣ 7 4 2

Your partner deals and opens 1NT. What would you respond if the strength were 12–14 points, and what if it were 15–17 points?

Answer: In either case you would respond 2♣ because it is clear that you would prefer this hand to be played in hearts or spades, particularly if partner has four cards in either. Notice that the hand contains a perfectly sensible rebid whatever partner responds, even 2◊.

If opener rebids either 2♡ or 2♠, showing a four-card suit, then whether his opening no-trump were weak or strong, you would put him to four in that suit.

As you learned in hand 9, responder can use this 2♣ bid on any strength of hand provided he wants to investigate a major-suit fit and that he has a sensible rebid available, whatever the answer to his question.

(Bids: 2♣ in either case)

12 ♠ J 9 7 2
    ♡ 10 8 6 4
    ◊ J 7 6 5 3
    ♣ –

Your partner deals and opens 1NT. What would you respond if the strength were 12–14 points, and what if it were 15–17 points?

Answer: This is another hand on which, whatever the strength of the opening no-trump, two things are clear: firstly it won't run to a successful game contract; and secondly, it is quite horrible for play in no-trumps. The final question, then, is whether or not it contains a sensible course of action if you bid 2♣ to see whether opener has a four-card major suit, and the answer to this, too, is yes.

If opener shows either four hearts or four spades by his rebid you will pass, knowing that he is likely to be far happier in a four-four trump fit than in no-trumps. If he bids 2◇ to deny a four card major, then again you will pass. The less length he has in hearts and spades, the better fit he is likely to have for diamonds, and your pass will only be leaving him in the suit in which you could have made a weak take-out in the first place.

(Bids: 2♣ in either case)

13 ♠ K J 6 ♡ Q 9 6 2 ◇ Q J 5 ♣ A 7 4	You deal and open 1NT (12–14 points), to which partner responds 2♣. What would you rebid?

Answer: Partner's 2♣ is a conventional request to you to show whether or not you have a four-card major suit, so your rebid is 2♡.

Had you held four spades instead of four hearts you would have rebid 2♠ and with both majors containing four cards you would show hearts first, which is the modern method of handling this type of holding.

Had you held an extra two points you would not have opened 1NT on this hand unless the agreed strengths were 15–17 points. In that case your response to a 2♣ bid from partner would have been exactly the same – these bids operate over any agreed strength of 1NT opening.

(Bid: 2♡)

14 ♠ Q 10 6 ♡ A 9 7 ◇ Q J 5 ♣ K J 7 2	You deal and open 1NT to which your partner responds 2♣. You correctly rebid 2◇ to deny a four-card major suit and he now bids 3♡. What would you bid?

Answer: Obviously partner's 2♣ was bid in the hope that he would find you with a four-card heart fit. Now that you have said you can't oblige he is doubtful about going on to 4♡ and is *asking* your opinion. In other words, his 3♡ is now highly invitational, but not forcing.

With your good opening no-trump (13½ points is very far from minimum) and ♡ A–x–x, an excellent fit, accept the invitation by raising him to 4♡.

(Bid: 4♡)

15 ♠ K J 8	There is no law against opening
♡ Q 9 6	1NT with a five-card suit, partic-
◊ Q 7	ularly when it is a minor. You open
♣ A J 9 6 5	1NT and partner responds 2♣.
	What would you rebid?

Answer: Until responder takes some further action to clarify his bid, 2♣ must be taken as a request to show any four-card major suit held. Lacking one, the rebid is 2◊ which, as you can see, bears no relation to the actual diamond holding or, for that matter, to anything else in the hand. So the correct rebid here is 2◊.

Don't take it upon yourself to pass in this situation just because you have a weakish hand and a five-card club suit. Your partner may be good enough to put you straight to 3NT except that he has thought it wiser to investigate your major-suit holdings first.

(Bid: 2◊)

16 ♠ Q J 9 6 5 3	Your partner deals and opens 1NT
♡ 7	(12–14 points). What would you
◊ K 6 3	respond and what difference
♣ 8 4 2	would it make if you held six clubs
	instead of six spades?

Answer: Holding the hand as it is above, with six spades, you would make a weak take-out into 2♠, which would be passed by your partner. He will understand that you have a weak hand which you think will play better in spades than in no-trumps.

If your suit were clubs instead of spades you would still not want to let partner play in no-trumps but, if you understood the previous quizzes, you will realise that 2♣ is conventional and so can't be used as a weak take-out bid.

The way to deal with this is to bid 2♣ and, when partner makes his conventional response, either showing or denying a four-card major, take out again into 3♣, from which he will understand that your only asset is a long weak club suit.

(Bids: 2♠ and 2♣)

17 ♠ A Q 7
 ♡ K J 8 2
 ◊ A Q J
 ♣ A K 5

Your partner deals and opens 1NT. What would you respond if the agreed strength were 12–14 points, and what if it were 15–17 points?

Answer: Your 24 points plus partner's known minimum of 12 points comes to a total of 36, amply good enough for a small slam. But if you put him direct to 6NT he will certainly pass even if, as is possible, he has his maximum of 14 points, though you would have an odds-on chance of making a grand slam. Bid a *conventional* 5NT, which *orders* partner to bid 6NT even on the barest minimum for his bid, and asks him to bid 7NT on a maximum. The one thing he mustn't do, of course, is to pass 5NT!

Facing a 15–17 point no-trump you know that there can't be more than one knave missing from the combined hands, so bid a direct 7NT without even consulting partner on the way.

(Bids: 5NT and 7NT)

18 ♠ A
 ♡ K Q J 10 6 5 4 3
 ◊ A 7 2
 ♣ 5

Your partner deals and opens 1NT (12–14 points). What would you respond?

Answer: It's well within the bounds of possibility that partner's weak no-trump opening contains no aces, in which case you might as well play in a comfortable 4♡. But if he has even one ace, you want to play in a small slam, and if he has two, in a grand slam contract.

Bid 4♣, the conventional Gerber request, which is used in place of Blackwood when the opening bid has been either 1NT or 2NT. The responses are, to show no ace, 4◊ – in which case you would simply convert to 4♡; 4♡ to show one ace, when you would convert to 6♡; and 4♠ to show two aces, which you would convert to 7♡ (7NT at duplicate). Using this convention, any rebid *other than* 5♣, which asks for kings on the same step principle, is the 4♣ bidder's decision as to the best final contract, and should not be disturbed.

(Bid: 4♣)

19 ♠ K J 10 7 6
♡ A Q J 9 3
◇ 7 5
♣ 8

Your partner deals and opens 1NT (12–14 points). You correctly bid 2♣ to which he replies 2◇. What would you rebid?

Answer: Your 2♣ response was, of course, asking for any four-card major held by your partner, but he has replied that he has none. In spite of this, however, you feel sure the hand will play better in spades or hearts, whichever fits his hand best. After all, having opened 1NT he cannot have less than a doubleton in both, and may have three in both or one of them.

Bid a conventional 3◇, which requests opener to show you his *longer* major. That is, if he has a three-card and a two-card suit, he bids the three-card suit. If both are of equal length he should bid the stronger. Whichever he chooses, you will raise him to game.

(Bid: 3◇)

20 ♠ Q J 10 6
♡ Q J 9 8 5 4
◇ A 8
♣ 7

Your partner deals and opens 1NT (12–14 points). You respond 2♣ in the hope of finding a four-card fit but opener rebids 2◇. What would you bid?

Answer: Had opener bid 2♡ or 2♠ you would have put him straight to game in what you know to be a good fit. He has, however, denied a four-card major, which makes you very much less certain that a game is 'on', even with this highly distributional hand.

Over 2◇ bid 3♡, not a mere 2♡ which would now be a weak take-out which he would pass. 3♡ is non-forcing but highly invitational and opener will raise to 4♡ if he possibly can or, perhaps, convert to 3NT if the hearts are his weakest suit.

Such hands are very difficult to judge correctly, and you may be missing a game if you fail to jump direct to 4♡. Make one of your queens into a king and that would be your correct rebid.

(Bid: 3♡)

21 ♠ 9
♡ A J 10 8 6 5 2
♢ Q 8 5 3
♣ 6

Your partner deals and opens 1NT (12–14 points). What would you respond?

Answer: It is pointless to beat about the bush in any way here, specially as opener's possible minimum of 12 points added to your 7 points makes only 19, leaving the balance of 21 for your opponents. Your left-hand opponent may have an equally distributional hand, and you want to make it as difficult as you can for him to show it.

Bid an immediate pre-emptive 4♡, making it impossible for him to come into the auction below the four-level in spades or the five-level in a minor.

A similar pre-emptive jump to the five-level in a minor can also be made with a bit of added length or strength to compensate for the higher contract. Apart from obstructing the opposition, such hands have an excellent chance of making a successful contract just on their distribution.

(Bid: 4♡)

22 ♠ 10 9 5
♡ Q 10 7 4
♢ K 8 3
♣ 9 5 2

Your partner deals and opens 2NT (20–22 points). What would you respond?

Answer: Though you would pass a 1NT opening, either weak or strong, without a moment's hesitation, when partner opens 2NT you know he has a minimum of 20 points. The same arithmetic applies – with 25–26 points you want to be in game.

It's worth raising 2NT to 3NT even on 4 points, especially if the hand contains good intermediates or a five-card suit. Here, counting your two tens, you have 6 points, so raise to 3NT.

The rules for responding to 2NT openings are somewhat

different from those for responding to 1NT, and we shall be covering these for the remainder of this section.

(Bid: 3NT)

23 ♠ 8
  ♡ Q J 10 8 6 4 3 2
  ◊ 9 3
  ♣ 5 4

Your partner deals and opens 2NT (20–22 points). What would you respond?

Answer: There is no immediate weak take-out available when partner opens 2NT, so if you decide you must play in a suit rather than in no-trumps, you will first have to decide whether you want to play at the three-level, at game level, or whether you want to try for a slam. On this hand the suit length, even with only three honour points, makes you want to play in 4♡. So you bid it as a sign-off.

(Bid: 4♡)

24 ♠ –
  ♡ K Q 10 9 7 5 3
  ◊ K 7 6
  ♣ 7 5 4

Your partner deals and opens 2NT (20–22 points). What would you respond?

Answer: Compared with hand 23 above, this time you immediately feel at least mildly interested in a slam. *Without* slam ambitions you would sign off in 4♡. With mild slam ambitions, bid 3♡, and opener's rebid of 4NT will then be conventional.

(Bid: 3♡)

25 ♠ Q 9 7 5 4
  ♡ Q 8 7 3
  ◊ J 10 8 4
  ♣ –

Partner deals and opens 2NT (20–22 points). What would you respond?

Answer: As already mentioned, had opener started with 2♣ to which you had responded 2◊, you would treat his 2NT rebid in the same way except that you would allow for the known greater strength.

Here you would infinitely prefer a suit to a no-trump contract. As you could bid 2♣ over 1NT to investigate for a four-card fit, so now you can bid 3♣ to investigate for *any* fit. When the opening bid has been at this higher level, 3♣ requests opener to show his four-card suits *in ascending order* and, if his only four-card suit is clubs, to rebid 3NT.

So bid 3♣ and if partner responds 3NT, you will know he has at least a four-card club suit and can let him play in 3NT. If he responds 3◊ (his lowest-ranking, not necessarily his only four-card suit) try 3♡ which he can raise, convert to 3NT, or himself show spades.

(Bid: 3♣)

26 ♠ A J 9 ♡ K Q J ◊ K J 9 3 ♣ A Q 7	You deal and open 2NT, to which partner responds 3♣. What would you rebid, and would it make any difference if your diamond and club holdings were reversed?

Answer: You don't at this stage know whether your partner has a possible slam (if he can find the fit he hopes for) in mind, or whether he thinks a suit contract rather than one in no-trumps will be safer. It is only up to you to answer the question he has asked, which is what four-card suits you have.

As the hand is now you would respond 3◊ which is, as it happens, your only, not your lower ranking four-card suit and you would also bid 3◊ if you had either four hearts or four spades too, as you are required to bid your four-card suits in *ascending* order (the Baron convention).

Reversing your minor suits would give you a four-card club suit only, and you would rebid 3NT. With another four-card suit besides clubs, you would rebid in that.

(Bids: 3◊ and 3NT)

27 ♠ 9 ♡ J 9 8 7 6 3 ◊ 10 7 5 ♣ 5 4 2	Your partner deals and opens 2NT (20–22 points). What would you respond?

Answer: Compare this with hand 23, where you wanted to try for a game in spite of the weakness in honour points. Here you are far too weak to want to go as far as 4♡. The solution is to bid a conventional Flint 3◊, requesting opener to make a transfer bid of 3♡, which you will pass. This simple device gives you a means of getting out of a dangerous no-trump contract into a far safer suit part-score contract.

(Bid: 3◊)

28 ♠ J 9 8 7 6 3   Your partner deals and opens 2NT
    ♡ 9   (20–22 points). What would you
    ◊ 10 7 5   respond?
    ♣ 5 4 2

Answer: This is the same hand as 27 except that the major suits are reversed, giving you long weak spades instead of hearts. Bid 3◊, as you did before, and when your partner, as this requests, transfers to 3♡, convert to 3♠ which, if he knows the convention, he will pass.

Note, by the way, that if you hold a genuine diamond suit and slam ambitions, the way to cope with this is to make the 3◊ response which opener will take as a request to transfer to 3♡ and then, when he does this, convert to 3NT instead of accepting the three-level contract. Partner should get the messsage.

(Bid: 3◊)

29 ♠ K Q 9   You deal and open 2NT (20–22
    ♡ A Q 7   points), to which partner responds
    ◊ K J 7 4   3◊. What would you rebid, and
    ♣ A Q 10   what action would you take if he
                    then bid 3NT?

Answer: Simply follow partner's instructions, as his 3◊ response asks you to do, and make a transfer bid of 3♡. Most probably he has a long weak heart suit, so will then himself pass or, if his suit is spades, he will rebid 3♠ – which you will pass.

Should he rebid 3NT when you bid 3♡, he will be showing slam interest with a diamond contract in view. The least you can do is take the hint. Bid what must be a Blackwood 4NT and if by any chance he has no ace you can pass his 5◊ reply. If he has one ace, 6◊ must be a good proposition.

(Bids: 3♡ and 4NT)

30 ♠ A J 10
   ♡ A K 10 6
   ◊ A K 7 5
   ♣ K 8

You deal and open 2NT, to which your partner responds 3◊. What would you rebid, and would it make any difference if your two four-card suits were spades and diamonds or spades and hearts?

Answer: Generally, when partner asks for specific action it is wiser to heed his request, but exceptions do crop up. Here, for example, with a maximum opener and huge heart fit you feel that, even after his transfer request, you don't want to let him play in a mere 3♡. So make another conventional bid, a transfer to 3♠. If his suit is spades, as in hand 28, he will now pass, but if it is actually hearts, he will have to convert to this suit at the four-level.

If the hearts and spades were exchanged, you would transfer to 3♡ as requested, but if partner then himself took out into 3♠ you would raise to 4♠. In the third case, with both major suits heavily held in a maximum hand, refuse the simple transfer and rebid 3NT, forcing partner to take himself out at game-level into whichever suit he really holds.

(Bids: 3♠, 3♡ and 3NT)

Competition quiz

In competition against another player, one should answer the three questions in the **A** set, and the other the three questions in the **B** set on each page.

1A Your partner deals and opens 1NT (12–14 points). What would you respond?

	1	2	3
♠	K 9 7	♠ K 9 7	♠ K 9 7
♡	Q 3 2	♡ Q 3 2	♡ Q 3 2
◊	Q 7 5 4	◊ Q 7 5 4	◊ K 10 7 4
♣	A 6 3	♣ Q 6 3	♣ A 6 3

Answers:

Bid (2 points)	Reason (3 points)
1 2NT	Your combined count cannot be less than 23 points

and may be up to the 25 needed for game if opener has 14, not his minimum of 12 points. Bid an *invitational* 2NT.

2   No   Even added to opener's possible maximum of 14
    Bid points, the combined count can't be within the game range.

3   3NT As the combined count can't be less than 24½ points, this is well worth a direct raise to 3NT.

1B   Your partner deals and opens 1NT (15–17 points). What would you respond?

1 ♠ Q 7 2	2 ♠ Q 7 3	3 ♠ Q 7 2
♡ K 9 7 2	♡ K 6 5 2	♡ K 6 5 2
◇ A 6 3	◇ Q 4 3	◇ Q 7 3
♣ Q 7 5	♣ Q 7 5	♣ 9 7 6

Answers:

Bid		Reason
(2 points)		(3 points)

1   3NT The combined count cannot be less than 26 points, ample for game, so bid it direct.

2   2NT The invitational raise, in the hope that partner is better than minimum, in which case he will go to 3NT.

3   No   The combined values can't reach game requirements,
    Bid and you have no ambitions towards a suit contract anyway.

2A   Your partner deals and opens 1NT (12–14 points). What would you respond?

1 ♠ Q 9 7 4	2 ♠ Q 9 7 4 3 2	3 ♠ 9 8
♡ K 8 3	♡ K 8	♡ Q 9 7 5 2
◇ J 9 7 5	◇ J 9 7 5	◇ 7 6
♣ 10 9	♣ 10	♣ K 9 7 3

Answers:

Bid		Reason
(2 points)		(3 points)

1   No   Your hand is too weak to raise no-trumps or to
    Bid suggest the alternative of a suit contract.

2   2♠   This is an immediate weak take-out, which opener is

expected to pass. Clearly this hand will be best played in a low spade contract, and not in no-trumps.

3   2♡   Another weak take-out, even though you have only a five-card suit. An opening no-trump must contain at least a doubleton heart, probably to an honour, which will make 2♡ a safer contract than 1NT with two worthless doubletons in the hand.

2B   Your partner deals and opens 1NT (15–17 points). What would you respond?

1	♠ K 9	2	♠ A J 10 7	3	♠ 9 8 7 5 4 3
	♡ Q 7 3		♡ J 9 8		♡ –
	◇ Q 9 8 7 6 3		◇ A 8 3		◇ J 9 7 4
	♣ 8 4		♣ 10 9 8		♣ 10 9 8

Answers:

Bid	Reason
(2 points)	(3 points)

1   2◇   It makes no difference that the opening no-trump is strong – this hand will play better in a low-level diamond contract, so make a weak take-out.

2   3NT   A very suitable hand to play in no-trumps and simple arithmetic tells you that this should be at game level.

3   2♠   Another example of a weak take-out. Don't leave partner to struggle in 1NT when you may even make 2♠!

3A   Your partner deals and opens 1NT (15–17 points). What would you respond?

1	♠ K J 8 6 3 2	2	♠ 8 7	3	♠ A Q 7
	♡ J 9 5		♡ 10 9 5		♡ K Q 6
	◇ A 8		◇ A K J 9 7 4		◇ K J 10 6 5 4
	♣ 10 6		♣ 10 6		♣ 4

Answers:

Bid	Reason
(2 points)	(3 points)

1   4♠   You have ample points to want to play in game but would prefer this to be in spades, not no-trumps. Bid 4♠ as a sign-off.

2   3NT You have no wish to play in 5◇ so it would be
          pointless to bid 3◇ on this hand. Bid what you think
          will be the best contract!

3   3◇   This time you personally would prefer to play in a
          diamond contract, which you announce by the 3◇
          game force. This hand may well run to a diamond
          slam.

3B Your partner deals and opens 1NT (12–14 points). What
        would you respond?

1 ♠ 10 8 4	2 ♠ 9	3 ♠ K J 8 6 3 2
♡ 9 7	♡ A Q 5	♡ J 9 5
◇ A K J 9 7 4	◇ K Q 7	◇ A 8
♣ 10 6	♣ K Q 10 6 5 4	♣ 10 6

Answers:

Bid	Reason
(2 points)	(3 points)

1   2◇   Almost the same hand as **3A**, 2, but worth no more
          than a weak take-out when facing a maximum of 14
          points.

2   3♣   Almost the same as **3A**, 3, and also worth a game-
          forcing take-out of 3♣ which may well lead to a slam,
          so make the slam invitation of 3♣. If opener rebids
          3NT, pass.

3   2♠   The same hand as **3A**, 1, but worth no more than a
          weak take-out when facing a 12–14 point no-trump.
          Note the need for accuracy in all the no-trump open-
          ing bids, as the responses are based on a knowledge of
          the maximum and minimum values held.

4A Your partner deals and opens 1NT (15–17 points). What
        would you respond?

1 ♠ K 7 6	2 ♠ K 7	3 ♠ K 7 6
♡ A Q 5 2	♡ A Q 10 9 7 3	♡ A 10 8 7
◇ A J 4	◇ A 6 4	◇ A 5 4
♣ A K 8	♣ A K	♣ K J 6

Answers:

Bid	Reason
(2 points)	(3 points)

1   5NT   Your 21 points plus partner's minimum of 15 come to 36 points, ample for a small slam. But if partner has his maximum there should be a good play for the grand slam. Bid 5NT asking him to go to 6NT with only 15 points and to 7NT with more, or with suit length somewhere.

2   4♣   Although a point weaker than 1, here there is a six-card heart suit. Get on immediately with the Gerber investigation into aces and kings. 4♣ will surely get a 4♡ 'one ace' reply, and 5♣, if the answer is 5♠ showing both the missing kings, should lead you straight to 7♡, which may be a little safer than 7NT.

3   3NT   15 plus even 17 only come to 32 points, not enough for a small slam without suit length, so just bid the game.

4B   Your partner deals and opens 1NT (12–14 points). What would you respond?

1 ♠ K J 6	2 ♠ A J 9 7 5 4 3	3 ♠ K J 5
♡ A Q 5 2	♡ 6	♡ A J 7
◇ A J 4	◇ 7 2	◇ A J 6
♣ A K 8	♣ Q 6 3	♣ K Q J 4

Answers:

Bid	Reason
(2 points)	(3 points)

1   6NT   Your 22 points plus partner's 12 come to 34 points, good enough for a small slam. But even if he has 14, it only comes to 36 points, not enough for the grand slam, so bid 6NT direct.

2   4♠   A pre-emptive jump bid which partner is expected to pass. You might even make it!

3   4NT   Inviting opener to bid 6NT if maximum or even with a good quality 13 points. Otherwise he may pass.

5A   Your partner deals and opens 1NT (12–14 points). What would you respond?

1 ♠ J 9 7 3	2 ♠ K 9 8 4	3 ♠ A K 7 4
♡ J 7 6 4 2	♡ J 10 8 6	♡ Q 3
◇ 9 3 2	◇ 5	◇ K 10 9
♣ 6	♣ Q 6 5 4	♣ J 6 4 2

Answers:

Bid	Reason
(2 points)	(3 points)

1   2♣   This hand will surely play better in hearts or spades if partner has a four-card fit for either. Bid 2♣ to ask him, and rebid 2♡ if he responds 2◇.

2   No   The essence of this 2♣ fit-finding bid is that you
      Bid   should have some sensible bid to make on the next round, especially if you don't get the answer you hope for from partner. Here, if he bids 2◇ to deny a four-card major, what can you say next? So pass and hope for the best!

3   2♣   With ample points to raise to 3NT anyway, you would prefer a spade contract if partner has a four-card fit.

5B   Your partner has opened 1NT (12–14 points), to which you have responded 2♣. What would you rebid if he now bid 2◇, and if instead he bid 2♡?

1 ♠ J 8 6 4 3	2 ♠ K 9 8 4	3 ♠ K 4 3
♡ J 10 9 5	♡ J 10 8 6	♡ A K 7 4
◇ 9 8 3	◇ 10 8 6 5 3	◇ Q 6 2
♣ 4	♣ –	♣ K 10 9

Answers:

Bids	Reasons
(1 point each)	(1½ points each)

1   2♠   You could have made a weak take-out into 2♠ immediately except that you took your chance to ask whether opener had four cards in either major.

      No   You have discovered a four-four fit which is what you
      Bid   hoped to do. Leave well alone.

2   No   You could have made a weak take-out into 2◇ except

Bid that you asked first if he had a four-card major suit.
No Having found a four-card heart fit, again leave well
Bid alone.
3 3NT With ample points for the raise, put partner to game.
3◇ Now you have a known four-four heart fit, offer
partner the choice between 3NT and 4♡ (SID).

6A Your partner deals and opens 1NT (12–14 points). What
would you respond?

1 ♠ A J 10 7	2 ♠ J 8 5 3	3 ♠ K J 8 4
♡ A Q 9	♡ J 2	♡ A Q 2
◇ 10 7 4 2	◇ 8	◇ Q J 7
♣ 8 6	♣ Q 9 8 5 4 2	♣ Q 10 8

Answers:

| Bid | Reason |
| (2 points) | (3 points) |

1 2♣ You would prefer to see this hand played in spades if
partner has a four-card suit – ask him.

2 2♣ Take your chance to ask if partner has a four-card
spade suit. Both here and in 1 you have a sensible
rebid if he replies 2◇ or 2♡.

3 3NT An ideal hand for play in no-trumps and it can't make
opener's up to slam requirements, so just bid game
direct.

6B You have responded 2♣ to partner's opening no-trump
(12–14 points). What would you rebid if he now bid (a) 2◇,
and (b) 2♠?

1 ♠ 8 6	2 ♠ J 8 5 3	3 ♠ K Q 10 6
♡ A J 10 7	♡ J 2	♡ 9 3 2
◇ A Q 9	◇ 8	◇ A J 9
♣ J 5 4 2	♣ Q 9 8 5 4 2	♣ K 7 5

Answers:

| Bids | Reasons |
| (1 point each) | (1½ points each) |

1 3NT It's a pity opener hasn't got a four-card heart suit, but

with 12½ points you must put him to game in no-trumps.

3NT Partner's 2♠ denies four hearts as well, so he *won't* remove 3NT to 4♡. At least you know he has a spade stop.

2   3♣ Show that your original 2♣ was largely based on a long weak club suit.

No The known four-four spade fit is likely to be safest, so
Bid don't bother with your long clubs this time.

3   3NT Partner has less than four spades or hearts, but you can't play below game-level with 14 points in your hand.

3♢ Having discovered the spade fit, offer partner the choice of 4♠ or 3NT (SID).

7A You deal and open 1NT to which partner responds 2♣. What would you rebid?

1 ♠ K 10 9	2 ♠ K 10 9 4	3 ♠ K 10 9
♡ Q 8 7 5	♡ A Q 7 5	♡ Q 8 7
◇ Q J 8	◇ Q J 8	◇ Q J 8
♣ A Q 3	♣ J 6	♣ A Q 3 2

Answers:

Bid   Reason
(2 points)   (3 points)

1   2♡ Answering the question you have been asked, and showing your four-card heart suit.

2   2♡ Again answering the question, but showing the heart suit first. From this you will see that a rebid of 2♠ denies four hearts, though a rebid of 2♡ does not deny four spades.

3   2♢ It makes no difference that your hand is maximum for your 1NT opening – just answer the question, which is whether or not you have a four-card major suit.

7B Carrying the bidding of the same three hands a stage further, as opener, what would you bid next in each of these sequences?

1 1NT–2♣	2 1NT–2♣	3 1NT–2♣
2♡–3♡	2♠–2NT	2◊–3♠
?	?	?

Answers:

Bid (2 points)	Reason (3 points)
1 4♡	Responder is inviting a game now that he has discovered a four-four heart fit. With a maximum for your opening bid, accept the invitation.
2 3♠	Presumably responder, who has now shown lack of interest in a heart fit, bid 2♣ in the hope that you would show spades. You *have* spades, as well as a hand which you are willing to play in 3NT if you must, but you would prefer spades. Give partner the choice.
3 4♠	Responder is strongly *inviting* a game contract in spite of your lack of a four-card spade suit. With your good quality opener and excellent three-card spade fit, go to 4♠.

8A You deal and open 1NT. Partner responds 2♣ and you rebid 2◊. What would you bid if he next bid 3♡?

1 ♠ K 7 2	2 ♠ K 7 2	3 ♠ K J 2
♡ Q 2	♡ Q 2	♡ Q 10 2
◊ K 8 7 5	◊ K 8 7 5	◊ K 8 7
♣ K J 6 2	♣ A Q 6 2	♣ A J 10 9

Answers:

Bid (2 points)	Reason (3 points)
1 No Bid	Partner is strongly *inviting* a game contract, but nothing about your hand makes you want to accept.
2 3NT	With a maximum opening and your weakest suit hearts, accept the invitation to bid a game, though in no-trumps.

3   4♡   Again perfectly willing to accept the invitation to bid
            game, though this time, with excellent heart support.
            Tell partner this will suit you if it is what he prefers.

8B On the same three hands as above, what would you, as
        opener, rebid in the following sequences?

        1 1NT–3♡   2 1NT–4♣   3 1NT–3♠
        ?   ?   ?

Answers:

Bid   Reason
(2 points)   (3 points)

1   3NT As the 3♡ bid is forcing to game you have no option
          but to bid again. Deny better than a doubleton heart
          with 3NT.

2   4♡   This is, of course, the response to partner's Gerber
          request to show aces. 4♢ would deny an ace, and 4♡
          shows one ace.

3   4♣   Technically an advance cue-bid in this position shows
          four-card trump agreement and a maximum no-trump
          with the ace of the suit bid. But a bit of common sense
          must be used – a player who can force in spades will
          be more than satisfied with ♠K–J–x in support, and
          with two tens you were really rather over strength for
          1NT in the first place.

9A Your partner deals and opens 1NT (15–17 points). What
        would you respond?

        1 ♠ K 10 8 6 5   2 ♠ K 10 8 6 5   3 ♠ K 10 8 6 5
           ♡ Q J 9 8 4   ♡ Q J 2   ♡ Q J 9
           ♢ 7   ♢ 7   ♢ 7 3
           ♣ Q 2   ♣ 10 9 6 3   ♣ K 10 4

Answers:

Bid   Reason
(2 points)   (3 points)

1   2♣   A less likely-looking hand for a happy no-trump
          contract would be difficult to find. Ask your partner if
          he can give you a fit for one of your majors.

2	2♠	With an unsuitable shape for play in no-trumps and insufficient strength to bid 2NT or 3♠, make a weak take-out into your five-card suit.
3	3♠	You have the values to raise to game, but would prefer the hand to be played in spades, so say so.

9B

On hand 1 above what would you bid next in the sequence:
1NT–2♣
2◇–?

2 ♠ K 10 8 6 5
♡ Q J 7 2
◇ 7
♣ 10 9 6
1NT–2♣
2♠–?

On hand 3 above what would you bid next in the sequence:
1NT–3♠
3NT–?

Answers:

Bid (2 points)	Reason (3 points)	
1	3◇	The hand is still highly unsuitable for play in no-trumps so you ask partner, with a conventional 3◇, to show his *better* major, i.e., three-card ahead of doubleton, and with two of equal length, to show the stronger.
2	3♠	Although low in honour strength, this hand is distributionally strong, and if partner is maximum could easily run to game in the known 5–4 spade fit. Invite him.
3	No Bid	Partner already knows that you have a spade suit but this will be his poorest suit – no better than a doubleton. If he decides 3NT will be better than 4♠, respect his decision.

10A Your partner deals and opens 2NT (20–22 points). What would you respond?

1 ♠ Q 10 8 3
♡ K 9 4
◇ 9 8 6
♣ 8 5 3

2 ♠ Q 10 8 3
♡ K J 4
◇ K J 8 7
♣ A 9

3 ♠ Q 9 8 6 5 4 3
♡ 9 7
◇ A 6
♣ 5 3

Answers:

Bid		Reason
(2 points)		(3 points)

1   3NT Facing a known minimum of 20 points, you have ample for a raise to 3NT, and no reason to prefer a suit contract.

2   6NT Your 14 points plus opener's known minimum of 20 come to 34, good for a small slam, but even if he has 22 points it will make a very sticky proposition of the grand slam.

3   4♠   There is no immediate weak take-out of a 2NT opening, so any response commits the partnership to game. Bid 4♠ as a sign-off.

10B Your partner deals and opens 2NT (20–22 points). What would you respond?

1	♠ K 9 3	2	♠ 7 4	3	♠ Q 10 8 6
	♡ A 7 5 4		♡ J 10 8 6 5 3		♡ K 9 7 2
	◇ Q J 8		◇ 9 6 2		◇ J 8 5 4
	♣ Q 10 7		♣ 8 4		♣ 7

Answers:

Bid		Reason
(2 points)		(3 points)

1   4NT Your 12 points plus partner's known minimum of 20 come to 32, but if he has his maximum of 22 points there should be a good chance of making a small slam. Bid a quantitative, *not* conventional, 4NT inviting him to go to 6NT if maximum.

2   3◇   This is the Flint conventional bid, asking partner to make a transfer bid of 3♡ which you intend to pass. This is your way of making a weak take-out into a major facing a 2NT opening.

3   3♣   This, facing 2NT, asks partner to show his four-card suits in *ascending* order, in the hope of finding a suit fit. If he has only one four-card suit, he will bid 3NT.

11A You deal and open 2NT, to which partner responds 3♢.
What would you rebid?

1	♠ A J 9 2	2	♠ A 7	3	♠ A Q J 10
	♡ A 10		♡ A Q J 10		♡ A 10 9 8
	♢ K Q J 7		♢ A K 8		♢ A K 8
	♣ A Q 6		♣ A 10 9 8		♣ A 7

Answers:

Bid	Reason
(2 points)	(3 points)

1   3♡   Responder's 3♢ is a conventional request to you to transfer to 3♡, which he will probably pass. But if his long weak suit is spades, he will 'correct' to 3♠.

2   3♠   Responder's 3♢ is still a request to you to transfer to 3♡ but with your maximum opener and strong heart fit you don't want him to play in a mere 3♡. Your 3♠ allows him to pass if spades is his suit, but otherwise he will have to 'correct' to 4♡.

3   3NT With this powerful maximum you want the contract to reach game in either major, and 3NT forces partner to pick the suit at the four-level.

11B You deal and open 2NT, to which partner responds 3♣.
What would you rebid??

1	♠ A 10 9	2	♠ A J 8 5	3	♠ A J 8
	♡ A J 8 5		♡ A 10 9		♡ A 10 9
	♢ K Q 10		♢ A J		♢ A Q 5
	♣ A Q 6		♣ A Q 6 5		♣ A Q 6 5

Answers:

Bid	Reason
(2 points)	(3 points)

1   3♡   3♣ is Baron requesting opener to show four-card suits in *ascending* order. (Some players use Stayman as over 1NT, so make sure you and your partner understand each other!)

2   3♠   With two four-card suits show the lower-ranking first unless it is clubs, which you can show later if expedient. 3♠, of course, denies a four-card red suit.

3   3NT This rebid shows that the *only* four-card suit held is clubs.

12A Your partner deals and opens 2♣, to which you respond 2♦. He then rebids 2NT. What would you bid next?

1 ♠ Q 9 4	2 ♠ Q 10 9 7 5	3 ♠ 9 5 3
♡ K 8 7 2	♡ J 9 8 6	♡ K 9 8 7 5 3
◇ 10 8 7	◇ 9 3	◇ Q 6 2
♣ 6 5 3	♣ 6 2	♣ 5

Answers:

Bid	Reason
(2 points)	(3 points)

1   3NT Opener's rebid shows 23–24 points instead of the mere 20–22 of a 2NT opening. You have ample to raise to game.

2   3♣ This bid is used in just the same way as facing a 2NT opening, that is, when you hope to find a suit rather than a no-trump contract.

3   4♡ Bid 4♡. This, of course, commits the partnership to game in hearts.

12B Your partner deals and opens 2♣, to which you respond 2♦. He then rebids 2NT. What would you bid next?

1 ♠ 9 8 6 5 4 3	2 ♠ 9	3 ♠ J 9 4
♡ 7 4	♡ 8 7	♡ 10 8 7
◇ 9 6 2	◇ Q 6 5	◇ 9 6 3 2
♣ 8 4	♣ K J 9 8 6 5 3	♣ 8 4 3

Answers:

Bid	Reason
(2 points)	(3 points)

1   3◇ This is the same Flint request to partner to transfer to 3♡ as you used in **10B**, 2. When he bids 3♡ you will take out into 3♠ which you expect him to pass.

2   3♣ Opener will take this as a request to show four-card suits in ascending order. If you can discover a club fit, this hand will run to a slam in that suit.

3   No Following a 2♣ opening, 2NT is the only opener's
     Bid rebid which can be passed below game level.

Section 4

Opener's Rebids

The basic rules

When partner has responded to an opening bid with a limit-bid, either a suit raise or no-trumps, opener's obligation to rebid is cancelled. He must now decide whether to pass, convert to what he considers a safer contract, or investigate towards a possibly better contract, either part-score, game, or even possibly slam.

If the response has been a change-of-suit which forces opener to speak again he should aim, as far as possible, at clarifying the shape and strength of his hand, though this often cannot be completed until a later round of bidding.

So, having studied the actual opening bids and the reasons for them in Section 1, let us now see how the auction gradually builds up to the final contract, each member of the partnership either denying, showing, or enquiring about values other than those already shown, if more information is still required.

1 *Following a responder's limit-bid:*

1♡–1NT   Responder has shown 6–9 points. According to strength, opener may pass 1NT, raise to 2NT on 17–18 points or to 3NT on 19 points. He may convert to two of his original suit (or more if strong) or show a second biddable suit which, at the two-level, would not be forcing.

1♣–1NT   Facing a 1♣ opening, 1NT shows 8–10 points, so
2♡   the above values may be reduced to allow for this.

1♠–2NT 3♡	This response has shown 11–12 points, and again opener may elect to pass, raise to 3NT, sign off in 3♠ or bid game. He can, if expedient, show a new suit which, at the three-level, is a one-round force. A 3NT response shows 13–15 points, and can obviously be passed or' converted to a four-level suit contract.
1◊–3NT 4◊	As this is below game level (being in a minor) the take-out is forcing, removing an existing game contract to one below game level. The 3NT response is not a shut-out bid and opener may, if strong, initiate slam investigations.
1♠–2♠ 1♡–2♡ 3◊–3♡ or 4♡	This weak limit-bid, showing four-card trump support and 6–9 points, can be passed or raised to game. Opener may also use a trial bid which shows doubt as to whether a game should be bid. It asks responder to convert to the original suit at the three-level on a minimum raise, to raise to game on a maximum or, on an intermediate hand, to let his decision rest on the trial-bid suit.
1♠–3♠ 4♣	Following a strong limit-bid at the three-level, opener can elect to pass, bid game direct or, if a slam now seems possible, start investigations. A new suit bid at this stage is a cue-bid, i.e. a control-showing bid, in reply to which responder should show his own lowest-ranking control.

2 *Following a change-of-suit response:*

On a minimum hand:

1♠–2◊ 2♠ or 2♡	A simple repeat of the suit opened is a sign-off rebid. A rebid in a second, lower-ranking suit no higher than the two-level shows a second biddable suit and promises no additional values. Neither rebid is forcing.

1◇–1♡ 1♠	A six-card suit should always be bid and rebid before a four-card suit *unless* the four-card suit is a major which can be shown at the one-level. Here, if
BUT 1◇–2♣ 2◇	6–4 in diamonds and spades, unless much better than minimum, opener should rebid 2◇ if the level is raised by a response of 2♣.

On a better-than-minimum hand:

1♡–1♠ 3♡	A jump rebid in the original suit is a strong though non-forcing limit-bid, showing seven playing-tricks at that suit. It also shows a six-card trump suit.
1♡–1♠ 2♠	A raise of responder's suit shows support in addition to the values for an opening bid. Always raise to the full value of the hand, i.e. to the three-level or even direct to game if strength permits. Though
1♡–1♠ 3♠ or 4♠	limit-bids, these last two are highly encouraging, not shut-out bids, showing that opener is not willing to play at any lower level.

On a strong hand:

1♡–1♠ 3♣	A jump rebid in a new suit is unconditionally forcing to game. A new suit bid at the three-level when responder has bid at the two-level is also
1♡–2◇ 3♣	forcing, so a player with a weakish hand must be careful not to get into a situation where there is no sensible rebid other than a forcing one, a factor which may have a bearing on the opening bid.

If responder forces:

1♡–3♣ 3♡	On single-suited hands, make a neutral rebid in the original suit, confirming suit length or, lacking a rebiddable suit, make the minimum available rebid in no-trumps unless strong enought to make a jump
1◇–2♡ 3NT	rebid in no-trumps, showing a hand good enough for a 2NT rebid in a non-forcing sequence.

1♡–3♣	With a second possible trump suit (biddable suit)
3◇	take the earliest chance, i.e. at the rebid, to show it.

1♡–3♣	A raise of responder's suit, particularly if this by-
4♣	passes the 3NT level, is highly encouraging. A jump rebid in opener's original suit shows a solid and self-supporting suit. (This applies at any time when a forcing situation is in being.)

3 *Opener's second round no-trump limit-bids:*

1♡–1♠	Facing a one-level response, 1NT = 15–16 points
1NT	2NT = 17–18 points
	3NT = 19 points.

1♡–2◇	Facing a two-level response, 2NT = 15–16 points
2NT	3NT = 17+ points.

1♡–1♠	A return to opener's original suit after his 2NT
2NT–3♡	rebid is forcing, requiring him to rebid 3NT or four
?	of the suit, in the knowledge that responder has no better than three-card trump support. (A responding hand with four-card trump support, particularly for a major, would have raised the suit initially to the three-level or now made a delayed game raise.)

4 *Swiss convention:* (one variation of many)

When the opening has been 1♡ or 1♠ an immediate response of 4♣ or 4◇ is conventional. Both show specific holdings in a hand which is under strength for a forcing take-out but good enough to demand at least a game contract. The raise to 4♣ shows four-card trump support, two aces, and 13–15 points, while the raise to 4◇ shows four-card trump support, three aces, and again, 13–15 points.

1♠–4◇	If opener merely repeats his suit at game level he
4♠	shows no interest in a possible slam. He may, however, bid an immediate 4NT which, as he
1♡–4♣	already knows the number of aces held by respond-
4NT	er, asks for kings on the Blackwood scale.

5 *Replies to responder's 'fourth suit forcing' rebids:*

1♡–1♠ 2♣–2◊	Responder is suggesting the values for a game contract with the accent on no-trumps. The fourth suit bid is a one-round force though it does not guarantee a further bid when made at the two-level. With a good stop in the fourth suit responder could himself rebid in no-trumps, but as he does not do so, he is seeking help from opener in the suit, in which he, responder, has only a partial guard.
1♡–1♠ 2♣–2◊ 2NT or 3NT	
1♡–1♠ 2♣–2◊ 2♡ or 2♠ or 3♣	Opener should give preference to a rebid in no-trumps if he holds a guard or partial guard in the fourth suit, bidding 2NT or 3NT according to strength. Failing ability to help with the fourth suit, opener must rebid as most appropriate to describe his hand further.
1♡–1♠ 2◊–3♣	A bid in the fourth suit made at the three-level promises the ability to make at least one further bid if needed to reach the best game contract. Opener should again rebid as appropriate to his hand, giving priority to a bid of 3NT if he holds the fourth suit stopped or partially stopped.
1◊–1♡ 2♣–2♠ 2NT–3♡	There are other more advanced sequences for use, for instance, when responder has a genuine strong two-suiter to show, and wants to play in one of his suits. Here his 3♡ rebid would indicate a strong spade-heart two-suiter, asking for opener's preference.

6 *After a strong two opening (2◊, 2♡, 2♠):*

2♡–2NT	The strong two is forcing for one round with a responder's negative of 2NT. Any positive response makes the sequence forcing to game.
2♠–2NT 3♠ 2♠–2NT	A simple opener's rebid at the three-level, either in the original or a new suit, is non-forcing, and though responder's only absolute obligation is to show preference, either by passing or 'correcting',

3♦	he will raise if he possibly can. Therefore, if wishing to reach a game at all costs, opener must make
2♥–2NT	either a jump to game, a jump rebid in a new suit
4♦ or 3♠	(forcing if below game level), or a forcing reverse. Responder is now responsible for seeing that the best game contract is reached.

2♥–4♥	When responder has made the ace-denial bid of a
4NT	jump to four of opener's suit, 4NT would, of course, be the Acol direct king convention, bypassing the request for aces and asking for kings on the Blackwood scale.

7 *After a two club opening bid:*

2♣–2♦	2♣ is unconditionally forcing to game unless open-
2NT	er rebids 2NT. Responder's negative is 2♦ and his second negative, if no more constructive bid is available, is 2NT. Opener's no-trump rebids have already been covered in Section 3.

2♣–2♦	The suit rebid is unconditionally forcing to game.
2♠	Thereafter the bidding develops naturally.

2♣–2♦	A jump rebid by opener is a conventional request to
3♥	responder to show any one ace he may hold in spite of his 2♦ denial, by a cue-bid. With no ace he should rebid 3NT.

8 *After a pre-emptive opening three-bid:*

3♥–3♠	A change-of-suit below game level is a one-round force. In a major, it shows a good suit and suggests game in it.

3♠–4♣	In a minor suggests a possible slam in *opener's* suit.

3♦–3NT	This is intended to play and opener should not 'rescue' in panic.

Exercises

1   ♠ 8 5   (a) 1♡–3♡ (b) 1♡–2NT (c) 1♡–3◊
    ♡ A Q 9 8 6 5   ?   ?   ?
    ◊ K 8
    ♣ J 10 6

Answers:

(a) With a minimum Acol light opener you refuse partner's invitation to go to game by passing his 3♡ limit-bid.

(b) The 2NT limit-bid, showing 10–12 points, leaves it up to you to judge the best final contract. Simply convert to 3♡.

(c) Partner is forcing you to speak again, so make a neutral rebid of 3♡ which merely confirms heart length.

                         (Bids: No Bid, 3♡ and 3♡)

2   ♠ K Q 9 7 3   (a) 1♠–2♣ (b) 1♠–2NT (c) 1♠–3♠
    ♡ A Q J 8 2   ?   ?   ?
    ◊ 9 6 3
    ♣ –

Answers:

(a) You opened 1♠ because you had a sensible rebid if partner responded in a minor, which is just what he has done. Rebid 2♡ as you had planned.

(b) Sometimes the auction takes a course you would have preferred it not to do, as it has done here. You can't leave partner to languish in 2NT, even though a new suit rebid at the three-level is forcing, so bid 3♡. After all, you have excellent 'shape', and a game in either major might well be successful.

(c) Again, basing your action on 'shape', you realise that it won't take much luck to make 4♠ a successful contract, so accept the invitation and bid it.

                         (Bids: 2♡, 3♡ and 4♠)

3   ♠ Q J 7   (a) 1♡–2◊ (b) 1♡–2NT (c) 1♡–3♡
    ♡ A Q 9 2   ?   ?   ?
    ◊ K 7 3
    ♣ K J 8   (Using a 12–14 point no-trump you rightly opened 1♡ instead of choosing a prepared 1♣.)

Answers:

(a) No need, of course, for a prepared opening when you have the strength for a sensible rebid in any situation, and when the response is 2◇ you rebid 2NT. This, over a two-level response, shows 15–16 points.

(b) Facing 10–12 points, which responder has announced, you simply raise him to 3NT. You have no ambitions towards a slam or a suit contract in preference to no-trumps.

(c) You could bid a direct 4♡, but there is no harm in telling responder that you have an evenly-balanced hand which was too strong for a 12–14 point no-trump opening bid. He will then judge whether to pass 3NT or 'correct' to 4♡.

(Bids: 2NT, 3NT and 3NT)

4	♠ A Q 9 6 2	(a) 1♠–1NT	(b) 1♠–2♡	(c) 1♠–2♣
	♡ K Q 6	?	?	?
	◇ Q J 5			
	♣ J 6			

Answers:

(a) Here you have to choose between letting your partner play in 1NT or taking out into 2♠ – either may be wrong. But as partner could not support spades he may well have something in clubs. Seven tricks in no-trumps may be easier than eight in spades, so pass.

(b) Give a simple raise to 3♡. Partner is certain to have at least a five-card heart suit and with your club weakness you can hardly bid no-trumps at this stage.

(c) Partner has shown a minimum of 8 points and a biddable club suit – your own weakness. Rebid 2NT to show 15–16 points, and leave it to partner to decide on further action, if any.

(Bids: No Bid, 3♡ and 2NT)

5	♠ A J 8 5	(a) 1♠–2♣	(b) 1♠–3♠	(c) 1♠–2◇
	♡ A Q 8 4	?	?	2♡–3♣
	◇ Q 10 3			?
	♣ Q 6			

Answers:

. (a) Partner has shown at least 8 points and a biddable club suit

– your own weakest holding. Rebid 2NT to show your balanced 'shape' and count, 15–16 points. (You could not consider opening 1NT as you were using 'weak'.)

(b) Never bid around the mulberry bush when you know the best final resting place. Simply go to 4♠ which you know will find four-card support and 10–12 points in partner's hand.

(c) Partner's 3♣ is fourth suit forcing, not showing clubs, which he could do by rebidding in no-trumps, but asking whether you can help with a partial club stop with a view to playing in no-trumps. Confirm his hopes by rebidding 3NT.

(Bids: 2NT, 4♠ and 3NT)

6   ♠ A 6 2   (a) 1♡–1♠ (b) 1♡–2♠ (c) 1♡–1♠
     ♡ A Q 10 8   2NT–3♠   3NT–4♡   2NT–3♡
     ◊ K J 6   ?   ?   ?
     ♣ Q J 8

Answers:

(a) You showed your full values by your original 2NT rebid, in spite of which responder only wants to play in spades. Respect his decision which is made in the knowledge that you have 17–18 points, by passing.

(b) When partner makes a game force you rebid 3NT, not just 2NT, to show your 17–18 points. When he next bids 4♡ your hand must be worth another try – bid 4♠ and leave it to him.

(c) Responder's 3♡, which is a return to the suit opened after the 2NT rebid, is forcing, and gives opener the choice between bidding 3NT or 4♡ in the knowledge that responder, lacking four-card heart support, could not bid this himself. This is a good hand for no-trump play, so rebid 3NT.

(Bids: No Bid, 4♠ and 3NT)

7   ♠ K J 6 2   (a) 1♡–2◊ (b) 1♡–1♠ (c) 1♡–2NT
     ♡ A Q J 5 3   ?   ?   ?
     ◊ Q 6
     ♣ K 5

Answers:

(a) Your hand is too good for a rebid of 2♡, and the general quality is not good enough for a reverse into 2♠. After all, you're not risking very much by a count-showing rebid of 2NT facing a partner who is good enough to make a change-of-suit response at the two-level.

(b) Raise direct to 4♠. There should be a play for game even if responder's hand is minimum, so you must not risk bidding only 3♠, which he might pass.

(c) Just raise quietly to 3NT, for which you have ample points. With at least one good honour card in all four suits, your hand must be invaluable to a partner who himself has 10–12 points.

(Bids: 2NT, 4♠ and 3NT)

8	♠ A Q 9 6 4	(a) 1♠–2◇	(b) 1♠–2♡	(c) 1♠–2NT
	♡ 5	?	?	?
	◇ K Q J 7 3			
	♣ A J			

Answers:

(a) Note first that you had no worries about whether to open 1♠ or 1◇ because clearly you were strong enough to have no rebid problems after a 1♠ bid. When partner responds 2◇, your second suit, rebid 3♣. This, being a new suit at the three-level, is forcing so you ensure yourself another chance to bid and, when you've heard responder's rebid, will more than probably go 'slamming'.

(b) Rebid 3◇, your second suit, which is again forcing, though with the lack of heart fit your sights are set on the best game contract rather than a slam at this moment.

(c) Show your second suit with 3◇ – forcing. This will warn responder that you are two-suited, which means a weakness in the other two suits. Leave him to judge the next move.

(Bids: 3♣, 3◇ and 3◇)

9	♠ A Q J 6 5	(a) 1♠–1NT	(b) 1♠–2♡	(c) 1♠–3NT
	♡ K 9	?	?	?
	◇ K Q 10 9			
	♣ A 5			

Answers:

(a) With 19 points opposite to a partner who can respond at all, even just 1NT, you want to be in game, and the sooner you get there without giving away the make-up of your hand, the better. Raise to 3NT.

(b) A whale of a hand, especially facing a partner who can respond at the two-level. Bid 3◇, forcing as it is a new suit at the three-level, on the way to the best game or possibly slam.

(c) Responder is showing 13–15 points. You have a powerful hand which must really now produce a slam. Bid 6NT direct as even if your combined total is only 32½ points, you have a five-card suit which adds to your strength.

(Bids: 3NT, 3◇ and 6NT)

10	♠ A Q 10 5	(a) 1♠–2♡	(b) 1♠–2♣	(c) 1♠–3◇
	♡ Q J 6	?	?	?
	◇ K Q 10 7			
	♣ K 3			

Answers:

(a) A one-round force of 3◇ is your rebid here. This hand is certainly going at least to game, but you are not yet sure whether the best denomination will be no-trumps, hearts, or even, depending on partner's rebid, a slam somewhere.

(b) Your count here justifies a rebid of 3NT when partner can respond at the two-level. Remember that a rebid of 2◇ would be a gross understatement of the hand – and might be passed anyway, as might 2NT – when you want to be in game.

(c) Raise to 4◇, firmly by-passing any suggestion of a 3NT contract. You are heading for a slam anyway, and it is possible that partner has forced in diamonds with the intention of supporting your spades later.

(Bids: 3◇, 3NT and 4◇)

11	♠ Q 9 2	(a) 1♡–1NT	(b) 1♡–1♠	(c) 1♡–2♠
	♡ A J 10 7	?	?	?
	◇ A Q 6			
	♣ K J 6			

(Using a 12–14 point no-trump you rightly opened 1♡ instead of choosing a prepared 1♣.)

Answers:

(a) Your hand is good enough to *invite* partner to advance to 3NT, by raising to 2NT. This shows 17–18 points which, if he has

8–9 points, has every chance of yielding a game.

(b) Make a limit-bid of 2NT, showing 17–18 points. This is, of course, non-forcing, though highly invitational.

(c) In (b) you were able to show your values with a bid of 2NT. Now, when partner has forced, he will never have any idea of your strength if you don't do better than that. Bid 3NT, which in this situation shows the same 17–18 points.

(Bids: 2NT, 2NT and 3NT)

12 ♠ A Q 10 8   (a) 1♠–2♡   (b) 1♠–2♣   (c) 1♠–3◇
    ♡ Q J 8   3◇–4◇   3NT–4♣   4◇–4NT
    ◇ K Q 10 6   ?   ?   ?
    ♣ K 3

Answers:

(a) This hand is almost identical to 10 though now the bidding is carried one round further. In this first sequence it must be clear that a slam is in the wind. Your partner will know that your forcing rebid of 3◇ may have been made on a short suit in spite of which he is raising – at the same time by-passing the 3NT level. Start investigations with 4NT.

(b) Your partner's 4♣ rebid, which removes an existing game contract into one below game, is forcing. Clearly he has long clubs and dislikes the idea of no-trumps. Raise him to 5♣.

(c) Your partner must have a big hand because, as an Acol player, he would only force the issue of a slam with greater strength than he needed for his original game force of 3◇. Just answer his Blackwood question as to how many aces you hold by bidding 5♣ to show one.

(Bids: 4NT, 5♣ and 5◇)

13 ♠ A Q J 6   (a) 1◇–2♣   (b) 1◇–1♡   (c) 1◇–1NT
    ♡ 7   ?   ?   ?
    ◇ A J 10 7 5 3
    ♣ 8 2

Answers:

(a) This hand is not strong enough for anything but a simple rebid in diamonds at the two-level. If you rebid 2♠ you would be showing strength you don't possess by reversing.

(b) You should always bid and *rebid* a six-card suit unless holding a four-card major suit which can be shown at the one-level. Here just this situation exists, so take your opportunity to rebid 1♠.

(c) You would be very ill-advised to do anything except take out into 2◊. Partner would surely have taken his opportunity to show a four-card spade suit at the one-level if he had it, so no spade fit has been missed and this is not a hand for a no-trump contract.

(Bids: 2◊, 1♠ and 2◊)

14	♠ A Q 10 9	(a) 1♡–1♠	(b) 1♡–2◊	(c) 1♡–3♡
	♡ A Q J 8 5	?	?	?
	◊ K 7 5			
	♣ 8			

Answers:

(a) The last thing you really expected was that partner would respond 1♠! However, even if his hand is completely minimum for this you feel there must be a good play for game. Bid 4♠ direct which is not a shut-out bid, because responder will realise that you were not willing to risk playing below game-level.

(b) Reverse into 2♠. This is a one-round force and responder will know that your hearts, because you bid them first, are longer than your spades, and that your hand is strong enough to be given preference to hearts at the three-level.

(c) Distributionally there may well be a slam on here. Try it out with a cue-bid of 3♠ which, in this context, shows first-round control of spades, not necessarily a suit. It is, of course, forcing.

(Bids: 4♠, 2♠ and 3♠)

15	♠ K 8 7 2	(a) 1♡–2♣	(b) 1♡–1♠	(c) 1♡–3♣
	♡ A K Q J 10 4	?	?	?
	◊ 7			
	♣ A 9			

Answers:

(a) Reverse into 2♠. This is a one-round force and responder will know that your hearts, because you bid them first, are longer than your spades. You can jump in hearts later.

(b) Raise direct to 4♠, not, as we have already seen, a shut-out bid, but showing that partner's response has hit the jackpot and that you are not willing to play below game-level. If responder himself is strong, he will take the hint and go slamming.

(c) When a forcing situation is in being, as it is here, a jump rebid shows a solid and self-supporting trump suit. Rebid 4♡, not as a stop bid but to encourage responder, who need not now worry about having possibly little or no heart fit.

(Bids: 2♠, 4♠ and 4♡)

16	♠ A Q	(a) 1♡–2♡	(b) 1♡–3♡	(c) 1♡–3♣
	♡ A 10 9 6 4 2	?	?	?
	◊ 9 5 4			
	♣ K J			

Answers:

(a) You are very doubtful about going to game facing a mere 2♡ raise. On the other hand your 'shape' is good and it won't take much to produce a game if responder's bits and pieces are in the right place – which particularly applies to diamonds. Ask him by making a trial bid of 3◊ – the suit you are worried about. You will meet partner's responses in the next section.

(b) This time you have no hesitation about going to 4♡. Note, by the way, that a rebid in diamonds now would be a cue-bid, not a trial bid.

(c) Rebid your hearts at the simple three-level, showing a rebiddable suit and no other biddable suit. A neutral bid.

(Bids: 3◊, 4♡ and 3♡)

17	♠ A Q 3	(a) 1♡–1♠	(b) 1♡–1NT	(c) 1♡–2◊
	♡ K J 7 3	?	?	?
	◊ J 9 2	(Using a 12–14 point no-trump, you		
	♣ A 8 7	opened one of your 4-card suit)		

Answers:

(a) Rebid 1NT, showing 15–16 points, in a hand just too strong to open 1NT.

(b) Partner has shown 6–9 points in a hand unable to support hearts. Just pass.

(c) On this somewhat flat hand be content with a simple rebid of 2NT, showing 15–16 points. Await developments, if any.

(Bids: 1NT, No Bid and 2NT)

18 ♠ A J 10 7   (a) 1♡–1NT (b) 1♡–1♠ (c) 1♡–2♣
    ♡ A Q 7 2   ?   ?   ?
    ◇ K J 6   (You opened 1♡ instead of 1♠ because
    ♣ A 5   this hand is very suitable for play in
              no-trumps *unless* responder raises
              hearts or himself bids spades.)

Answers:

(a) A rare type of hand, this, on which you want to make it easy for responder to raise hearts or show a spade suit. When he does neither you are sure a major-suit fit is missing and raise him to 3NT for which you have the values.

(b) This time responder comes up with a biddable spade suit. There might now be a slam on – test the market with a forcing 3♣; responder will know that this may be done on a short suit. Anyway, see what he bids next – you can always put him back into spades later.

(c) As responder has neither raised hearts nor bid spades, show your values by a jump to 3NT, the denomination you always fancied for this hand.

(Bids: 3NT, 3♣ and 3NT)

19 ♠ A Q 10 8 6 5   (a) 1♠–3♠ (b) 1♠–4♣ (c) 1♠–2♡
    ♡ K Q 4   ?   ?   ?
    ◇ K 6
    ♣ A 3

Answers:

(a) With this strong hand facing a 3♠ raise you must start thinking in terms of a possible slam. But go a little warily before committing yourself to a contract higher than 4♠ – investigate where partner's goodies lie by a cue-bid of 4♣, to which he will reply by showing his lowest-ranking first-round control.

(b) Partner has made a Swiss conventional response showing trump agreement, two aces, and 13–15 points. Bid 4NT asking for kings on the Blackwood scale – you've already been told about his aces, and want to be sure that, missing one ace between you, partner has the ♠K.

(c) As soon as partner mentions hearts, a guaranteed five-card suit, you start thinking of higher things. But you need more information. Bid 3♣ (a high reverse) showing a 16+ point hand and asking partner to clarify his own hand.

(Bids: 4♣, 4NT and 3♣)

20	♠ 10	(a) 1♡–2♡	(b) 1♡–2♣	(c) 1♡–4◇
	♡ K Q J 10 8 6	?	?	?
	◇ A K 2			
	♣ 7 5 3			

Answers:

(a) You could bid 4♡ and then find partner with a flat hand except for the ♠K and ♡A–x–x–x, in which case you might well go two down. If, however, he can help with either honours or a shortage in clubs, 4♡ becomes a good proposition. Ask him with a trial bid of 3♣.

(b) Show seven playing tricks with a 6-card heart suit by a jump rebid of 3♡. Partner will understand that you would like to be in game but that, for your money, this should be in hearts.

(c) Simply sign off in 4♡ saying that, in spite of your knowledge of what partner is showing by his Swiss 4◇, you have no wish to reach a slam contract. After all, he has not got the values for a forcing bid.

(Bids: 3♣, 3♡ and 4♡)

21	♠ 7	(a) 2♡–2NT	(b) 2♡–2♠	(c) 2♡–3♡
	♡ A Q J 10 8 5	?	?	?
	◇ A Q J 10 3			
	♣ 4			

Answers:

(a) Show your second suit, diamonds, at the lowest available level. Knowing that you have a strong two-suiter responder will try to help you into a game in the one he prefers, though he is not forced to bid again. If he gives you preference to 3♡ it would be worth trying 4♡.

(b) The 2♠ positive response makes the sequence forcing to

game. No need to hurry – just show your two-suiter by a rebid of 3◊.

(c) This positive response shows trump support and at least one ace or void. Bid 4◊ showing the cheapest first-round control, not necessarily a suit now that hearts are agreed, and await responder's rebid.

(Bids: 3◊, 3◊ and 4◊)

22   ♠ 7   (a) 2♡–2NT (b) 2♡–3♡ (c) 2♡–3NT
    ♡ A Q J 10 8 7   ?   ?   ?
    ◊ A K J 9 7 5
    ♣ –

Answers:

(a) You want to be in game in one of your red suits despite partner's negative response, so you must force him to speak again to tell you which of them he prefers. Rebid 4◊ and he must either 'correct' to 4♡ or raise to 5◊.

(b) Be a bit clever here – you greatly want to know if partner has the ♠A (a void is extremely unlikely on your hand). Cue-bid 4♣, your lower-ranking control. If partner has the ♣A he will know at least that this is duplication of values. If he bids 4◊, it will be showing a void, but if he bids 4♠ you can now investigate for the grand slam contract.

(c) Partner has 10–11 points but no biddable suit. 6♡ is not likely to depend on worse than a heart finesse, so bid it.

(Bids: 4◊, 4♣ and 6♡)

23   ♠ A K Q 9 4   (a) 2♡–3♡ (b) 2♡–2NT (c) 2♡–3NT
    ♡ A K J 8 7 3   ?   ?   ?
    ◊ 4
    ♣ 6

Answers:

(a) Partner's 3♡ is, of course, showing heart agreement and at least one ace or void. You can feel confident of no heart losers, spades should take care of themselves, so whether you go to a small or grand slam depends on whether he has one or two aces (he *might* have none and a spade void!) Bid 4NT to find out.

(b) You certainly want to be in a game, either in hearts or spades, so reverse into 3♠, which is forcing for one round. Partner must raise to 4♠ or correct to 4♡, whichever he thinks best in the knowledge that your hearts are the longer.

(c) Partner has 10–11 points so a slam might be on the map. But, from your point of view, 3NT is not a good idea. Rebid into 4♠ to see if partner has a fit for this suit.

(Bids: 4NT, 3♠ and 4♠)

24　♠ A K J 10 6 5 3　　(a) 2♠–2NT (b) 2♠–3♠　(c) 2♠–3NT
　　♡ K 7　　　　　　　　?　　　　　　?　　　　　　?
　　♢ 9
　　♣ K Q 6

Answers:

(a) With what is really only a minimum for the original 2♠ opening, simply rebid 3♠. Partner is under no obligation to bid again but, knowing how good your hand is, he may be able to put you to game when he would have passed a lesser opening bid.

(b) Partner has at least one ace or void, but he will have to make any slam try there is to be. Bid 4♠ and leave it to him to pass or bid on once he knows you have no extra values to show.

(c) This time partner has 10–11 points. Simply convert to 4♠ knowing that you probably have at least three aces to lose – partner must have some diamond honours and possibly the ♡Q.

(Bids: 3♠, 4♠ and 4♠)

25　♠ K 6 4　　　　　(a) 2♡–2NT (b) 2♡–3♡　(c) 2♡–4♣
　　♡ A K Q 10 8 7 4　?　　　　　　?　　　　　　?
　　♢ A 3
　　♣ 8

Answers:

(a) Just quietly rebid 3♡ and hope that responder, knowing you have at least eight playing tricks, will be able to put you to game.

(b) Responder has at least one ace or void, not necessarily *only* one ace or void, and a trump fit. It cannot do any harm to cue-bid your lowest (only) other control by bidding 4♢. If responder can show the ♠A there should be a good play for 6♡.

(c) As 2♡ is a forcing bid, a forcing situation is in being, so responder's 4♣ shows a long solid self-supporting club suit. Knowing he needs no support for this – and that you will be able to use it for discards if you won't allow him to play in clubs, get on with finding out if he has the ♠A too by bidding 4NT. If he does not have the ♠A, finish in 6NT.

(Bids: 3♡, 4♢ and 4NT)

26 ♠ A 10 9 6 5 3   (a) 2♠–2NT (b) 2♠–3♢ (c) 2♠–3NT
     ♡ A K J 8 7   ?   ?   ?
     ♢ A Q
     ♣ –

Answers:

(a) In spite of the strength of your hand you don't really want to be in game if partner has a Yarborough. Bid 3♡ showing your second suit. If he can possibly do so, partner will bid again, possibly to put you to 4♡ or 4♠, or just to 'correct' to 3♠.

(b) Responder can make a positive bid without the ace and queen of his suit, which he would not do if he had spade support to show at this stage – far more likely to be helpful than 3♢. The sequence is now forcing to game, so show your second suit – you can always put the contract back into diamonds.

(c) Here, not much caring for a no-trump contract, you can show your hearts over 3NT, leaving it to partner to choose between 4♡ and 4♠.

(Bids: 3♡, 3♡ and 4♡)

27 ♠ K Q   (a) 2♣–2♢ (b) 2♣–2NT (c) 2♣–2NT
     ♡ A K Q 7 5   ?   ?   3♡–4♡
     ♢ A K 9   ?
     ♣ A 6 3

Answers:

(a) A simple bid of 2♡, showing the best suit, makes the sequence forcing to game. At this stage responder will not know whether you have more than one suit, but that will develop later.

(b) 2NT is positive. For the moment simply show your heart suit and await developments.

(c) It is to be hoped that you did not notice the rebid in (c) before you had answered (b), as this is only a continuation of the same sequence. With the 2NT showing positive values, and now finding a heart fit, the least you can do is investigate a grand slam with 4NT. If responder has not got the ♠A he will surely have club honours to make 6♡ worth bidding.

(Bids: 2♡, 3♡ and 4NT)

28   ♠ A K Q J 10 6 2   (a) 2♣–2◊   (b) 2♣–2♡   (c) 2♣–2◊
     ♡ K Q 7   ?   ?   3♠–4◊
     ◊ K Q   ?
     ♣ A

Answers:

(a) If partner has just one red ace and nothing else, it would not give him a positive response to 2♣. A jump rebid by opener in this sequence now asks him to cue-bid it if he has one and, if not, to rebid 3NT. So rebid 3♠ and, if he bids 3NT to show no ace, convert to 4♠.

(b) Jump-rebid 3♠ to ask partner to cue-bid any ace he may hold – very hopeful now that he has given a positive response. If he has none, the worst that can happen is that you will play in 4♠, but he's got to have enough points to make up a positive, so will surely have one ace.

(c) This is a continuation of the sequence in (a). Partner has the ◊A which makes 6♠ the obvious contract.

(Bids: 3♠, 3♠ and 6♠)

29   ♠ A K Q J 10 6 5 2   First, what's the right opening bid
     ♡ –   here? Got it? Then:
     ◊ 6   (a) 4NT–5♣ (b) 4NT–5♡ (c) 4NT–5◊
     ♣ A K Q J   ?   ?   ?

Answers:

(a) Note the vital importance of discovering which ace, if any, responder holds. 5♣ denies any ace, so just convert to 6♠, the contract you expect to make.

(b) Here responder holds the useless ♡ A, so again just convert to 6♠. Note that responder must never disturb opener's rebid, whether this is at the five-level or higher.

(c) Now responder has the vital ◇ A, and nothing but a first-round ruff could defeat 7♠, so bid it.

(Bids: 6♠, 6♠ and 7♠)

30　♠ A 7　　　　　　(a) 2♣–2 ◇　(b) 2♣–2♠　(c) 2♣–4♣
　　　♡ A K 3　　　　?　　　　　?　　　　　?
　　　◇ A K Q J 6 5 4
　　　♣ 5

Answers:

(a) 2 ◇ is, of course, a negative response, so 3 ◇ is showing your suit, not raising responder's!

(b) A positive response with a biddable spade suit – not that you particularly want to play this in spades, but a diamond slam is a near certainty so get on with investigations via 4NT.

(c) Partner has a solid and self-supporting club suit, needing no help from you. If you are declarer you will be able to use it for discards of your losers, and if he is declarer your diamonds will serve the same purpose for him. So take your pick as long as you bid the grand slam, 7♣ or 7 ◇ or, if you are playing MP Pairs, you will want to go for 7NT.

(Bids: 3 ◇, 4NT, either 7♣, 7 ◇ or 7NT)

Competition quiz

In competition against another player, each in turn should answer a full page of six questions. As an added exercise, you might like to decide on the correct opening bid on each hand before going on to the scoring questions on rebids. You met the opening bids in Section 1, but note that no hand in this section is to be opened with a bid in no-trumps, from which you must assume that your agreed no-trump range is either too weak or too strong.

1A	1	♠ 9 3	2	♠ 9 3	3	♠ A Q 7 5
		♡ K J 8 5		♡ K J 10 7 2		♡ 8
		◇ A Q 10 7 4 2		◇ A K J 6 5		◇ K Q 6 3
		♣ 8		♣ 8		♣ K J 8 5

| 1◇–1♠ | 1♡–1♠ | 1◇–1♡ |
| ? | ? | ? |

Answers:

| Bid | Reason |
| (2 points) | (3 points) |

1   2◇   A simple rebid in your six-card suit, which was really your only excuse for opening.

2   2◇   With two adjacent suits you rightly opened one of the higher-ranking, leaving yourself a sensible rebid in the other.

3   1♠   You opened one of the suit below the singleton to give yourself a sensible rebid in any circumstances.

What would you bid next on the same hands in these sequences?

4	1◇–1♠	5	1♡–2NT	6	1◇–1♡
	2◇–2♡		?		1♠–2NT
	?				?

Answers:

| Bid | Reason |
| (2 points) | (3 points) |

4   3♡   When partner hits the jackpot with his second try, your 'shape' and trump fit make it worth the single raise.

5   3◇   You can hardly leave partner languishing in 2NT. Even though your new suit bid at the three-level is a one-round force, show it.

6   3NT   Never mind your singleton – this is in partner's suit. Your combined values should be at least 26 points.

1B 1 ♠ A Q 7 5   2 ♠ 5   3 ♠ A Q J 7 2
         ♡ K J 10 8   ♡ 9 5 4 2   ♡ A 10 9 4
         ◊ K Q 7 6   ◊ A K 6 3   ◊ K 3
         ♣ 7   ♣ A Q J 4   ♣ 7 5

         1♡–1♠   1◊–2♣   1♠–2◊
         ?   ?   ?

Answers:

Bid   Reason
(2 points)   (3 points)

1   3♠   You opened 1♡ to facilitate finding a possible spade
          fit. Counting distribution your hand, if played in this
          suit, is now worth 17 points, and you can raise to the
          three-level.

2   3♣   You opened 1◊, treating the hand as a minor two-
          suiter. A raise to 3♣, giving partner another chance, is
          enough.

3   2♡   With a weakish hand of 5–4 shape, open one of the
          five-card suit and, as long as you can do so at the two-
          level, rebid in your four-card suit, provided it is lower
          in rank than your original suit.

What would you bid next on the same hands in these
sequences?

      4 1♡–2♣   5 1◊–1♠   6 1♠–2♡
        2◊–2♡   2♣–2NT   3♡–3♠
        ?   ?   ?

Answers:

Bid   Reason
(2 points)   (3 points)

4   No   It sounds as if responder's hand were minimum, as all
     Bid he can do is give simple preference to hearts. Pass, and
          be happy to make a plus-score.

5   3NT Partner is making another try, showing 11–12 points
          as well as the biddable spade suit. This should make
          3NT a good proposition, even if your hearts are not
          very good. Partner has shown a guard in this suit,

which may even make your 7♡ valuable!

6   4♡   It's anybody's guess whether 4♡ or 4♠ will be safer on this hand, but you have a certain 5–4 heart fit, and certainly no better than 5–3 in spades.

2A

1	♠ A 7 5	2	♠ A J 10 3	3	♠ A Q 9 3
	♡ K 8 4 2		♡ K J 10 7		♡ K 8 4
	◊ Q 9 3		◊ A 6 4		◊ A J 8 6
	♣ A 8 4		♣ A J		♣ 7 2
	1♣–1♠		1♡–2♣		1♠–2♣
	?		?		?

Answers:

Bid	Reason
(2 points)	(3 points)

1   1NT   You opened a prepared 1♣, not being strong enough for the 15–17 point no-trump you are using. Make your rebid in no-trumps to make it clear to partner that you are not bidding on a long club suit.

2   3NT   You opened 1♡, to make it easy for partner to show a spade suit if he had one. Rebid 3NT, clearly the best denomination and what your hand is worth.

3   2◊   You opened 1♠ to facilitate your rebid, which it has done. Let the auction develop quietly on this modest hand by showing your second biddable suit.

What would you bid next on the same hands in these sequences?

4	1♣–1♡	5	1♡–1♠	6	1♠–2♡
	2♡–2NT		?		3♡–3NT
	?				?

Answers:

Bid	Reason
(2 points)	(3 points)

4   3NT   When responder bid 1♡, your four-card suit, it would have been senseless to rebid 1NT, as you did in 1 above. Now he is making another try, actually in the denomination you had in mind in the first place. Raise to 3NT.

5   4♠   Partner's 1♠ may have been minimum, but never

leave to him what you can do yourself. A spade game contract must be worth trying.

6   No   Don't disturb what looks like a perfectly good con-
     Bid   tract. Partner was not forced to speak again over your
          3♡, so he must have extra values to what he needed
          for his 2♡ bid.

2B	1	♠ A 10 9 6	2	♠ 8 5	3	♠ K Q 6
		♡ 7 3		♡ A 10 9 7		♡ K J 5 4
		◇ A Q 9 5		◇ K J 5		◇ A 6 2
		♣ K J 4		♣ A Q 5 2		♣ K 9 5
		1◇–1♡		1♣–1♠		1♡–2♣
		?		?		?

Answers:

Bid   Reason
(2 points)   (3 points)

1   1♠   Take it easy – if responder can't bid a second time you don't want to be in a high contract. If you bid 1♠, you can still play in 1NT, but if you bid 1NT the spade fit will be lost.

2   1NT   You opened 1♣ because 1♡ would have implied a five-card suit. Partner has shown his spade suit, so rebid 1NT to indicate what your hand is worth.

3   2NT   The 1♡ opening on this 16 point hand left you with no rebid problem. Now show your count and even distribution with a 2NT rebid.

What would you bid next on the same hands in these sequences?

4	1◇–1♡	5	1♡–2♠	6	1♡–2♣
	1♠–2♣		?		2NT–3♡
	?				?

Answers:

Bid   Reason
(2 points)   (3 points)

4   3NT   Partner's 2♣ is a 'fourth suit forcing' request, not showing a club suit, but asking whether you can help

to stop clubs for a no-trump contract. You can, especially as he will have a little something in clubs himself. Respond in no-trumps according to your values if you have the help he needs – in this case with 14 points, bid 3NT.

5   3♣   Although you rebid 1NT when partner responded 1♠, when he forces you should take this opportunity to show any possible alternative trump suit.

6   3NT The 3♡ rebid, a return to your original suit after your 2NT rebid, is forcing, and asks for your choice between 3NT and 4♡. Partner has only three hearts, or he would have made a 3♡ limit-bid in the first place or bid 4♡ now.

3A   1 ♠ Q 9   2 ♠ J 6   3 ♠ Q 8
        ♡ A K 7 4 3   ♡ A K Q 8 4   ♡ A Q J 7 5 4
        ◊ K 8 5   ◊ K J 5   ◊ K 5
        ♣ Q J 6   ♣ A 10 8   ♣ 10 9 8

        1♡–1♠   1♡–2◊   1♡–1♠
        ?   ?   ?

Answers:

Bid		Reason
(2 points)		(3 points)

1   1NT With 15–16 points and a stop in both unbid suits, 1NT is a more constructive rebid than an apparent sign-off into 2♡.

2   3♣   This is a one-round force (a new suit at the three-level) designed to get partner to clarify his hand. ♠J–x is not enough for a rebid in no-trumps and 3◊ might be passed when either 3NT, 4♡ or 5◊ can be made.

3   2♡   Simply sign-off in your own six-card suit. The hand has no future unless partner can bid again.

What would you bid next on the same hands in these sequences?

        4 1♡–2NT   5 1♡–1♠   6 1♡–2NT
           ?   ?   ?

Answers:

Bid		Reason
(2 points)		(3 points)

4   3NT Facing 11–12 points you must have ample values for game. Any contract can come adrift on the rocks of a misfit, but this is clearly your best resting-place.

5   3NT With 17–18 points, technically your rebid is 2NT, but you must take your excellent heart suit into account.

6   4♡   3NT is not an attractive idea on this hand so your choice is between signing off in 3♡ or going for game. If partner's 11–12 points are in the right place, 4♡ should have a good chance of success.

3B

1 ♠ A K J 6 4	2 ♠ K Q 6 3	3 ♠ A J 10 8 6 4
♡ 7 6	♡ A J 10 8 6	♡ 9 2
◇ J 10 8 3	◇ K 6	◇ A K Q 5
♣ A J	♣ A 5	♣ A
1♠–2♡	1♡–2◇	2♠–2NT
?	?	?

Answers:

Bid		Reason
(2 points)		(3 points)

1   2NT With 14 points your choice is between an underbid of 2♠ and 2NT, which requires 15 points. You actually have 14½ *and* a good five-card suit, which is adequate compensation.

2   2♠   This reverse is a one-round force showing a strong hand with longer hearts than spades. Partner will bid at least once more, if only to put you back to 3♡, but he will think in terms of bidding no-trumps if he has something in clubs.

3   3♠   The hand was too good for a simple 1♠ opening, but was somewhat minimum for 2♠. Just rebid your long suit at the lowest available level.

What would you bid next on the same hands in these sequences?

4 1♠–2◇	5 1♡–2◇	6 2♠–3♠
3◇–3♠	2♠–3♡	?
?	?	

Answers:

Bid	Reason
(2 points)	(3 points)

4   4♠   By his 3♠ rebid partner is showing that, lacking the four-card spade support needed for an immediate 3♠ limit-bid, he thinks his hand worth another try. He probably has ♠Q–x–x and, with your diamond fit, this makes the game contract worth bidding.

5   4♡   Partner is showing simple preference for hearts and lack of a club stop in reply to your forcing 2♠ reverse. Even so, it should be worth bidding the game, as he has already shown at least 8 points.

6   4♣   Partner has shown a trump fit and at least one ace *or* void. If this is in hearts he will show it in reply to your cue-bid, after which 6♠ becomes an excellent proposition.

4A	1 ♠ A Q J 3	2 ♠ K J 9	3 ♠ A J 10 8 5 4
	♡ A K Q 6 2	♡ Q J 5	♡ 8 5 2
	◇ Q 4	◇ A Q 10 6	◇ K J
	♣ 7 5	♣ A 8 4	♣ A Q
	1♡–2♣	1◇–1♠	1♠–2♠
	?	?	?

Answers:

Bid	Reason
(2 points)	(3 points)

1   2♠   Strong enough to open 1♡ and reverse into 2♠, a one-round force. This gives information as well as asking partner to clarify his own hand further.

2   2NT   This, of course, shows a reasonably balanced hand

with 17–18 points, leaving partner to judge the best final contract.

3   3♡   This is a trial bid – a one-round force – telling partner that in view of his weak response you are doubtful about bidding 4♠ direct. It also asks if he can give any 'help' in hearts, your own weak spot.

What would you bid next on the same hands in these sequences?

4	1♡–2♣	5	1◊–2♣	6	1♠–2♠
	2♠–2NT		?		3♡–3♠
	?				?

Answers:

Bid   Reason
(2 points)   (3 points)

4   3NT   When asked to clarify his hand, partner has neither supported spades, given preference to hearts, nor rebid clubs. He is showing a stop in diamonds, so 3NT becomes a reasonable proposition.

5   3NT   When partner can respond at the two-level, showing at least 8 points, you are too good to bid a mere 2NT, showing a maximum of 16 points which might be passed out.

6   No   Partner is either completely minimum for his 2♠ raise
     Bid   or has no help for you in hearts. Be content where you are.

4B

1	♠ K Q J 10 7 2	2	♠ A Q 9 8 6	3	♠ A 9 3
	♡ A K 7		♡ A Q J 8 4 3		♡ 4
	◊ 9		◊ 7 4		◊ A J 5
	♣ K 5 2		♣ –		♣ K Q J 10 6 5
	1♠–2◊		1♡–2♣		1♣–2♣
	?		?		?

Answers:

Bid   Reason
(2 points)   (3 points)

1   3♠   This jump rebid shows that you are only a trick short

of a strong two bid, i.e. that you have seven playing tricks at spades, with at least a six-card spade suit.

2   2♠   You may be low in honour points for a forcing reverse but the 'shape' is magnificent, and the hand is only a little short of a strong two opening.

3   2♦   5♣ is a long way to go if 3NT can be made and there is a good chance that partner has the ♣A in his humble response. 2♦ is a minor-suit trial bid, different from a trial bid when there has been a major-suit opening. Now you *show* a stop and ask responder if he can show one in return.

What would you bid next on the same hands in these sequences?

4	1♠–2♠	5	1♡–2♣	6	1♣–2♣
	?		2♠–3♣		2♦–2♡
			?		?

Answers:

Bid	Reason
(2 points)	(3 points)

4   4♠   Never bid around the mulberry bush when you know where you are going. No need for anything but a direct 4♠ here, as even if partner can only raise to 2♠ you want to be in game.

5   3♠   Having opened 1♡, when you bid *and rebid* spades, partner will know that this suit, being rebiddable, is at least a five-card suit and that, therefore, your hand is at least 6–5 in hearts and spades – in that order.

6   3NT Relying on your clubs and on your partner to provide a stop in hearts, go for the no-trump game. He can always take out if he thinks it wisest.

5A	1	♠ A Q J 5 3	2	♠ K Q J 7 5 2	3	♠ A Q J 8 6 3
		♡ 7 2		♡ 6		♡ A K 10 7 4
		♦ 9		♦ –		♦ 10 6
		♣ A Q J 8 4		♣ K Q 9 8 7 3		♣ –
		1♣–1NT		1♣–1♡		2♠–2NT
		?		?		?

Answers:

Bid	Reason
(2 points)	(3 points)

1   2♠   You can't leave partner languishing in 1NT! As his hand is limited by his 1NT response, your spade rebid is not a forcing reverse, and he may pass if he thinks this wisest.

2   1♠   Yes, you open 1♣ on two equal-lengthed black suits whether they are four, five or six cards long! When you rebid in spades partner will know that your clubs are at least as long, if not longer than your spades. If he can't bid again voluntarily you don't want to be in a high contract.

3   3♡   Just that much stronger than **4B**, 2. Make a simple rebid in your second suit – not forcing.

What would you bid next on the same hands in these sequences?

4 1♣–1NT	5 1♣–1♡	6 2♠–2NT
2♠–3♠	1♠–2◇	3♡–4♡
?	?	?

Answers:

Bid	Reason
(2 points)	(3 points)

4   4♠   Partner's 1NT has shown 8–10 points, and now that he knows you have a black two-suiter he is encouraging you when he need not do so. In spite of your low count, bid 4♠ on 'shape'.

5   3♠   Partner's fourth-suit-forcing 2◇ is exploring for a no-trump contract (the last thing you want), from which you can safely infer that his responding hand is not minimum. Your jump bid in spades is forcing and will indicate your 'shape' and will make it clear that your hand is almost completely black.

6   No Bid   Partner's original 2NT makes any thought of a slam a poor idea. Pass, and be happy to have discovered a trump fit.

146   *Acol-ite's Quiz*

5B 1 ♠ A K J 8 5 2   2 ♠ 7   3 ♠ A J 9 7 5
       ♡ A Q 10 9 8 7   ♡ A K J 10 3   ♡ K J 9 7 5 4
       ◇ 8   ◇ A K J 7 6 2   ◇ J 6
       ♣ –   ♣ 5   ♣ –

       2♠–2NT   2◇–2NT   1♠–2♣
       ?   ?   ?

Answers:

Bid   Reason
(2 points)   (3 points)

1   4♡   You want to be in game at all costs and a simple rebid
         of 3♡ would not be forcing. Partner's only obligation
         now is to decide which suit you should play in, by
         passing 4♡ or 'correcting' to 4♠.

2   3♡   This reverse is forcing so there's no need to jump.
         Partner must raise to 4♡ or 'correct' to 4◇, showing
         his preference. He might even be able to show real
         diamond preference with 5◇.

3   2♡   This hand is the odd man out, not strong enough for a
         two-bid and not even strong enough for an opening
         1♡ with a reverse into spades. It is an example of an
         exception to the rule that you should bid the longer
         suit first, but all you risk is getting preference to
         spades which you don't really prefer!

What would you bid next on the same hands in these
sequences?

       4 2♠–4♠   5 2◇–4◇   6 1♠–2♣
       ?   ?   2♡–3♣
                                               ?

Answers:

Bid   Reason
(2 points)   (3 points)

4   5◇   This is a canny bid. You are now interested specifically
         in the ♡K, and partner already knows *you* know he
         has no aces. Cue-bid 5◇ and, with the ♡K, he will
         cue-bid it in reply. He won't push you into the slam by
         cue-bidding the ♣K if he has that and not the ♡K.

5 5◇ As partner has announced no first round controls, no thoughts of a slam arise.

6 No You've said your little all – if partner is solely club-
   Bid minded, the lower the contract stays, the better!

6A 1 ♠ A Q 9 7 3   2 ♠ A 6   3 ♠ A Q J 2
       ♡ K Q 6   ♡ A K Q J 7 4   ♡ A K Q J 10 9
       ◇ 8 7 2   ◇ K 6   ◇ A 7
       ♣ K 5   ♣ A Q 3   ♣ A

       1♠–4♣   2♣–2◇   2♣–2♠
       ?   ?   ?

Answers:

Bid   Reason
(2 points)   (3 points)

1   4♠   Partner's 4♣ was Swiss, showing two aces, good trump support, and 13–15 points. Even if he has 15 points, you are under strength for a slam, so just convert to 4♠.

2   2♡   A simple rebid in your best suit, which is forcing to game.

3   5NT If partner has the values for a positive response all you need is to be sure they aren't all in the minor suits – for the grand slam he must have the ♠K. 5NT is a grand slam force in reply to which, with none of the top three spade honours he must rebid 6♣ (which you would convert to 6♠) and with one, which can only be the king, he must bid six of the agreed trump suit, which you would raise to seven. Note that you are willing to give up your hearts to play in spades.

What would you bid next on the same hands in these sequences?

4 1♠–4♣   5 2♣–2◇   6 2♣–2◇
   4◇*–4♠   2♡–2NT   2♡–4◇
   ?   ?   ?
   *A cue-bid.

Answers:

Bid		Reason
(2 points)		(3 points)
4	No Bid	Partner's rebid of 4♠ suit shows that he has nothing extra to show. Be content with the game contract.
5	4♡	Give up and settle for the game contract – partner has made not only one, but two negative bids.
6	7♡	4◇ shows a long solid and self-supporting diamond suit missing the ace. Your hearts are so self-supporting that you can afford to play in this suit knowing that all your losers will go away on his diamonds. Bid 7♡ at rubber bridge because you score an additional 150 points for the five top trumps, and 7NT at duplicate.

6B

1	♠ A Q 9 7 3	2	♠ A 6	3	♠ A Q 7
	♡ K Q 6		♡ K 6		♡ A K Q 10 8 6
	◇ A 7 2		◇ A Q 3		◇ A 7 2
	♣ K 5		♣ A K Q J 7 4		♣ A
	1♠–4♣		2♣–2◇		2♣–2◇
	?		?		?

Answers:

Bid		Reason
(2 points)		(3 points)
1	4NT	By now you know what partner's Swiss 4♣ means. For a successful slam it is vital to know whether he also has a king. Bid 4NT which, as he has already said that he holds two aces, asks for kings on the Blackwood scale.
2	3NT	Conventionally this shows an evenly-balanced hand of 24 or more points, but a 3♣ rebid risks the second negative of 3NT coming from partner which might be disastrous. 3NT from your hand, with the lead coming up to you, is an odds-on bet.
3	2♡	The simple rebid in your own suit, forcing to game.

What would you bid next on the same hands in these sequences?

4	1♠–4♣	5	2♣–2♡	6	2♣–2◇
	4◇–4♠		?		2♡–4◇
	?				?

Answers:

Bid	Reason
(2 points)	(3 points)

4   4NT   You don't often try for a grand slam after a mere one-level opening, but partner has the two missing aces and good trump support. If he also has the two missing kings you must be able to make at least 6♠.

5   3♣   After the positive response just rebid your own good suit. The inherent danger of partner being the first to bid in no-trumps is now nothing to worry about.

6   7◇   Your hearts are not as self-supporting as in **6A**, 6, though responder's 4◇, of course, still shows long, solid and self-supporting diamonds missing the ace. Let him play in diamonds, as he will surely be able to ruff out your hearts if the suit doesn't fall.

Section 5

Responder's Rebids

The basic rules

When responder's rebid in an uncontested auction has been reached there have already been three bids, and responder should be well on the way to knowing whether to settle for a part-score, game, or even a slam. If opener's rebid has been a sign-off or a limit-bid, then responder is under no obligation to rebid himself. If he does so, therefore, it must be at least to improve, if not to increase the existing contract, though it may also be up to him to make further investigations as to the best final resting place.

1 *On a minimum hand:*

1♠–1NT 2♠–No	When opener has made a sign-off rebid, responder may – and almost always should – now pass. Alternatively if opener has shown two suits, responder must show his preference, either by passing the second bid suit or returning opener to his first suit at the lowest available level.
1♠–1NT 2♡–No or 2♠	
1♡–1♠ 2◊–2♠	A repeat of responder's own suit at the lowest available level is also a sign-off bid, showing weakness except for that suit and no particular liking for either of opener's suits.

♠–2♠   If opener makes a trial bid in spite of responder's
3◇–3♠   weak limit-bid, a minimum responding hand is
          shown by a simple rebid of opener's suit.

2 *On a better-than-minimum hand:*

1♡–1♠   Responder may make another forward move as, for
2◇–2NT   example, rebidding in no-trumps to show a count
          of 10–12 points and a stop in the unbid suit.

1♡–1♠   A jump in responder's suit is encouraging, showing
2◇–3♠   a good suit and no particular interest in either of
          partner's suits.

1♡–1♠   A raise of partner's second suit or a jump bid in
2◇–3◇   partner's first suit constitutes a raise rather than
or 3♡   mere preference and also shows a better-than-
          minimum hand.

1♠–2♠   Responder must also give a positive response to
3◇–4♠   opener's trial bid if his original raise were made on
          better than a minimum.

3 *Responding hands with game hopes:*

1◇–1♡   On hands worth an attempt to reach a game con-
2◇–2♠   tract responder may reverse, a one-round force
          which should be understood by opener as an
          invitation to bid no-trumps if he holds the fourth
          (unbid) suit stopped.

1♡–2◇   A new suit rebid at the three-level is also a one-
2♡–3♣   round force which may conveniently be used for
          exploration with a no-trump contract in view.

1◇–1♡   A bid in the fourth suit is the fourth suit forcing
2♣–2♠   convention, used for exploration towards no-
          trumps or to ask opener to clarify his hand. Made at
          the two-level, it does not guarantee a further bid if
          responder judges that the best contract has now
          been reached. Opener, in replying, should give
          priority to a rebid in no-trumps at the appropriate

level if holding a partial stop in the fourth suit. The fourth-suit bid is a one-round force.

1♡–1♠
2◇–3♣

This again is fourth-suit-forcing, except that at the three-level it guarantees a further bid if game has not been reached by opener's rebid.

1♡–2◇
2♠–?

If opener reverses, showing strength, responder should aim at clarifying his hand, giving priority to a rebid in no-trumps if holding the unbid suit covered.

1♡–3♡
4♣–?

Following the highly invitational limit-bid of 3♡, a new suit rebid by opener is a cue-bid. Responder should show his lowest-ranking first-round control in reply.

1♡–1♠
2NT–3♡

A return to opener's original suit after his 2NT rebid is forcing, requiring opener to bid 3NT or the suit game contract. As responder did not bid 3♡ in the first place or 4♡ on this second round, opener can expect no more than three-card trump support.

4 *On strong hands:*

1♡–1♠
2♡–4♡

1♡–1♠
2NT–4♡

A delayed game raise sequence may be used when a hand is too strong for an initial limit-bid at the three-level, as this might be passed out and a game missed, and not strong enough for an immediate forcing take-out. Compare the last example in 3 above, where responder would rebid 4♡. In the third example sequence, responder will have a strong hand, but may have only three card trump support which can be deemed sufficient once opener's suit has been *re*bid.

1♠–2◇
2♠–4♣

Even if responder has been unable to force initially, a subsequent jump bid in a new suit is still unconditionally forcing to game.

1♡–1♠ 2♡–2NT or 3NT	Count-showing no-trump limit-bids may also be made on suitable hands though a possibly more constructive initial response was made on the first round.
1♠–4♣ 4◇–? 1♡–4◇ 4NT–?	When a responding hand has the requirements for a Swiss response of 4♣ (four-card trump support, two aces, and 13–15 points), opener's rebid of 4◇ is a cue-bid following either the 4♣ or 4◇ Swiss response, any subsequent rebid of 4NT by opener asks for kings, not aces which are already known, on the Blackwood scale.
1♠–3◇ 3♡–4◇ 1♠–3◇ 3♠–4♠ 1◇–3♣ 3◇–3NT	When responder is strong enough to make a game force on the first round, he should aim at clarifying his hand at his rebid. He knows that the auction will be kept open to game anyway. He may repeat his own suit, show support for opener's suit or perhaps rebid in no-trumps. Unless holding better than a minimum for his initial force, once having announced the strength to force, he should leave slam investigations to opener.

5 *Rebids following a strong two opening bid:*

2♡–2NT 3♡–4♡ or No	After a negative response, opener's simple rebid in his original or in a second suit is not forcing. Responder may judge whether to pass or, even on a weak hand, make another move, knowing the strength held by his partner. If partner shows a two-suiter, responder must show preference, either by passing, correcting to the first-bid suit, or even possibly raising one or the other. These bids are a matter of common sense and judgement.
2♠–2NT 3♡–No or 3♠ or 4♡ or 4♠	
2♡–2NT 4◇–4♡ or 5◇	Opener's jump rebid in a new suit is forcing to game, and responder must either correct to the first suit or raise the second.
2♡–2NT 3♠–?	A reverse rebid by opener is also forcing, and requires the same treatment.

2♡–3♣	Any positive response makes the sequence forcing
3♡–?	to game, and responder simply makes the most sensible rebid available.

6 Rebids following a 2♣ opening:

2♣–2◇	2NT is not forcing and responder may pass on a
2NT–?	completely worthless hand. Similarly he is under no obligation to take action if opener rebids 3NT.

2♣–2◇	A suit rebid by opener is unconditionally forcing to
2♡–?	game. Responder's second negative is 2NT which he must bid if common sense tells him he has no more constructive bid available.

2♣–2◇	A jump rebid by opener asks responder to cue-bid
3♡–?	any one ace he may possibly hold, in spite of his 2◇ negative.

2♣–2♡	After any positive response to 2♣ the bidding
2♠–?	proceeds naturally.

Exercises

Throughout this section you have already responded to your partner's opening bid, and in some cases to his subsequent bid. Now you have to decide on your rebid in each of the sequences shown.

1	♠ 9	(a) 1♡–2♡	(b) 1♠–1NT
	♡ K 10 8 4	3◇–?	2♣–?
	◇ Q J 10 6		
	♣ 9 6 5 3		

Answers:

(a) Partner's 3◇ is a trial bid. It asks whether you are maximum or minimum for your 2♡ raise or, if you are doubtful, whether you can give any help in diamonds, a spot where he has some weakness. You are nearly maximum for your original bid and, in addition, you have 'help' in diamonds, so bid 4♡ direct.

(b) Opener's spades must be longer than his clubs, so he is

almost certainly 5–4 in the two suits. You have, therefore, reached a sure 4–4 trump fit and, with no higher ambitions, you should pass this no-forcing rebid.

(Bids: 4♡ and No Bid)

2   ♠ K J 7 4   (a) 1♡–1♠   (b) 1♡–1♠
     ♡ Q 9 3   2♣–?   2NT–?
     ◇ K Q J 8
     ♣ 8 3

Answers:

(a) With an honour to help in the suit opened by your partner and an excellent stop in the unbid suit, diamonds, rebid 2NT. This shows 10–12 points just as it would have done as an initial response except that, at that stage, clubs appeared to be wide open.

(b) Clearly you have the values to bid a game, but are not sure whether 3NT or 4♡ will be best, the latter probably being the safer if partner has a five-card heart suit. Bid 3♡, a *forcing* bid (a return to opener's suit after his 2NT rebid), requiring him to choose. He will know that you have neither the four-card trump support required for an immediate raise to 3♡, nor the values for a delayed game raise, with which you would now bid 4♡ yourself.

(Bids: 2NT and 3♡)

3   ♠ 9 7 4   (a) 1♠–1NT (b) 1◇–2◇ (c) 1♠–1NT
     ♡ A Q 7   3◇–?   3♣–?   3◇–4◇
     ◇ J 9 6 3   4♠–?
     ♣ 7 4 3

Answers:

(a) Opener's jump rebid is forcing which, in view of the fact that you could do no more than bid 1NT, must mean that he has a strong two-suiter. Do the obvious, which is to give him a raise to 4◇.

(b) 3♣ is a trial bid in the minors, and at least a one-round force. Rather than showing a weakness, as in 1(a), it shows a guard and asks whether partner can show another guard with the idea of getting into a final no-trump game contract. So bid

$3\heartsuit$, showing your strength in this department, which may be just what partner wants to hear.

(c) A game contract has now been reached so you are under no obligation to bid again and, indeed, should not do so. Three-card support for partner's bid and rebid suit is adequate and you have no slam ambitions.

(Bids: $4\diamondsuit$, $3\heartsuit$ and No Bid)

4　♠ K 10 9　　　(a) $1\heartsuit$–$3\heartsuit$　(b) $1\spadesuit$–$2\clubsuit$　(c) $1\spadesuit$–$2\clubsuit$
　　♡ 10 9 8 3　　　　 $3\spadesuit$–?　　　 $2\heartsuit$–?　　　 $4\clubsuit$–?
　　◇ 8
　　♣ A Q J 9 4

Answers:

(a) $3\spadesuit$ is a cue-bid which means that your partner, in the light of your strong $3\heartsuit$ limit-bid, is now thinking in terms of a possible slam. Make a return cue-bid of $4\clubsuit$, not showing a club suit but showing first-round control of clubs, after which leave any further pressing to him.

(b) Never leave partner to do what you can do yourself – everything about your hand now looks good, so raise to $4\heartsuit$.

(c) Doubtless you've found partner with a four-card club fit, but as he bid spades first that must be his longer suit, that is, at least a five-card suit. Put him to $4\spadesuit$ and then, of course, follow up any further action he may possibly take.

(Bids: $4\clubsuit$, $4\heartsuit$ and $4\spadesuit$)

5　♠ Q 9 6 4　　　(a) $1\heartsuit$–$2\heartsuit$　(b) $1\spadesuit$–$2\spadesuit$　(c) $1\diamondsuit$–$1\heartsuit$
　　♡ Q 10 8 3　　　　 $3\diamondsuit$–?　　　 $3\heartsuit$–?　　　 2NT–?
　　◇ 7 5 3
　　♣ K 5

Answers:

(a) $3\diamondsuit$ is a trial bid again. However, if partner is looking for either a maximum for your original raise or help in diamonds, you have neither. Sign-off in $3\heartsuit$.

(b) $3\heartsuit$ is also a trial bid, but there is a difference when this is made in a *second major*. Partner may have a four-card heart suit, that is, he may be 5–4 in spades and hearts. As long as the rest of the hand justifies giving encouragement rather than a sign-off, you should raise the second major with a four-card fit for it, so here you should bid 4♡. With 'help' in the second major in the form of a shortage you would, of course, make the appropriate rebid in the original suit – for example, exchange your hearts and clubs, and you should bid 4♠ in response to the 3♡ trial bid.

(c) Notice how the same hand can demand positive or negative action according to partner's obvious requirements. Here, even if he has his 18 point maximum making a combined total of 25 points, you have little with which to help him to go to town. Unless you are badly in need of points in a match, you would do best to pass.

(Bids: 3♡, 4♡ and No Bid)

6	♠ K 9 6 4	(a) 1♡–1♠	(b) 1♡–1♠	(c) 1♡–1♠
	♡ A 8	2♣–?	2♢–?	2NT–?
	♢ Q 3 2			
	♣ K J 10 7			

Answers:

(a) If partner can help with even a partial stop in diamonds, 3NT will surely be the best contract. *Ask* him with a fourth-suit forcing 2♢ which, as you will see, does *not* show a diamond suit.

(b) Unless so two-suited that you can't even think in terms of a no-trump contract, never go bidding away against your partner in your two suits whilst he bids the other two. Compare with (a) above where you asked about his diamond holding. Here show your excellent clubs and full values by bidding 3NT.

(c) Just raise to 3NT, for which clearly there must be ample points between the combined hands.

(Bids: 2♢, 3NT and 3NT)

7	♠ Q 5 4	(a) 1♡–2♣	(b) 1♠–3♣	(c) 1♠–3♣
	♡ 8	2♡–?	3♠–?	3♢–?
	♢ A Q J 8			
	♣ A Q J 7 5			

Answers:

(a) Note that because of the complete lack of heart fit, you content yourself with a simple 2♣ on the first round. When partner can only rebid 2♡ you bid 3◊, a responder's reverse as well as a new suit at the three-level and, therefore, forcing. With anything at all in spades your partner, who *must* bid again, will go into no-trumps, or bid 3♠ as fourth-suit forcing, asking you to help.

(b) As ♠Q–x–x is by no means a lack of fit for partner's suit you force with 3♣ on the first round. When partner only rebids a neutral 3♠ raise to 4♠. Don't yourself go pressing on as he should be capable of taking the hint if he has anything like a decent hand.

(c) This time, with the almost incredible diamond rebid, you can afford to be the one to press on. Go straight into a Blackwood 4NT, as you are perfectly prepared to play in a diamond slam if partner has the necessary controls.

(Bids: 3◊, 4♠ and 4NT)

8	♠ A Q 10 9 7	(a) 1◊–1♠	(b) 1◊–1♠	(c) 1◊–1♠
	♡ A Q 9 7 4	2◊–?	1NT–?	2♣–2♡
	◊ 8			2NT–?
	♣ Q 3			

Answers:

(a) You can't afford not to try to reach the best game contract, so in spite of partner's apparent diamond sign-off, force with 3♡.

(b) If you are using a weak no-trump, partner is showing 15–16 points and again you want to find the best game contract. Bid 3♡.

(c) When partner's rebid was 2♣ you took your opportunity to bid a fourth-suit-forcing 2♡ which partner would take as a request to go into no-trumps if holding a partial guard in hearts. His confirmation that he has something in hearts can only mean that you have a reasonable heart fit, so bid 4♡ – no one could expect you to want to play this hand in no-trumps.

(Bids: 3♡, 3♡ and 4♡)

9   ♠ A J 7 2   (a) 1♡–2♣   (b) 1♠–4♣   (c) 1♠–4♣
     ♡ 8 5 3   2♠–?   4◇–?   4NT–?
     ◇ 6
     ♣ A K 8 5 4

Answers:

(a) Note that partner has made a forcing reverse into 2♠, showing a strong hand with longer hearts than spades. The least you can do is bid 4♠, not as a shut-out, but to confirm the fit and your own excellent hand.

(b) Your 4♣ was Swiss, showing a four card trump fit, two aces, and 13–15 points. Partner's 4◇ is a cue-bid to which you reply by showing your own *cheapest* control.

(c) Again, of course, your 4♣ was Swiss, and partner, therefore, already knows the number of aces you hold – two. He is now asking immediately if you have any kings in addition, and you respond 5◇ on the Blackwood scale to show one.

(Bids: 4♠, 4♠ and 5◇)

10   ♠ A K 7 4   (a) 1♡–4♣   (b) 1♣–1♡   (c) 1♣–1♡
     ♡ J 10 9 6   4NT–?   2♣–?   2◇–?
     ◇ A 9 3
     ♣ Q 8

Answers:

(a) Your 4♣ was Swiss, showing a four-card trump fit, two aces, and 13–15 points. Just as in 9 (c) above, partner is not asking something he already knows, so again he is asking for kings, if any, and you respond 5◇ to show one, on the Blackwood scale.

(b) Go straight into 3NT without further ado. Notice, by the way, that you bid the lower-ranking of your two four-card majors first.

(c) Whether or not an opener's reverse in the second minor is unconditionally forcing or not is a controversial point. However, only on the weakest of weak responding hands would you think of passing. Bid your full values with 3NT and leave it to opener to decide whether or not to go slamming.

(Bids: 5◇, 3NT and 3NT)

11 ♠ A Q 9 6 3   (a) 1♠–3◇   (b) 1♡–1♠   (c) 1♡–1♠
    ♡ 10 7   3♡–?   2♡–?   3♡–?
    ◇ A K 9 6 2
    ♣ 6

Answers:

(a) Having rightly forced on the first round don't bid your hand twice at this stage. Just rebid 3♠, knowing that partner is capable of understanding that you have the values for a force. You may well end up in a grand slam contract here.

(b) Not suitable for a first-round force when partner opened 1♡, you must still make an effort to reach the best game contract. Bid 3◇, a new suit at the three-level and, therefore, a one-round force. If partner can only rebid 3♡ raise him to 4♡, but if he rebids 3NT, stand it.

(c) Partner has shown a hand worth seven playing tricks in hearts, but note that he did not show eight playing tricks by opening 2♡. Don't be selfish – just raise to 4♡.

(Bids: 3♠, 3◇ and 4♡)

12 ♠ J 9 8 6   (a) 1♡–1♠   (b)   No   (c)   No
    ♡ Q 7 3   2♣–?   1♣–?   1♣–1NT
    ◇ A 9 4   2♠–?
    ♣ J 10 7

Answers:

(a) Just give a simple preference bid of 2♡, not raising but, with even better heart than club support, putting him back to his first suit. His 2♣, of course, is not forcing, but it is still up to you to take action if appropriate.

(b) Having already passed – note this important fact – it is better to show a count of 8–10 points than to show this poor spade suit and risk a pass from partner.

(c) Opener is *not* making a forcing reverse, as your 1NT is a strictly limited bid. He is, in fact, showing a black two-suiter, almost certainly five-five, which he doesn't fancy for a no-trump contract. Your hand is minimum for your first response and a good fit has been discovered, so pass.

(Bids: 2♡, 1NT and No Bid)

13 ♠ K Q 10 7 4   (a) 1♡–1♠   (b) 1♡–1♠   (c)   No
   ♡ K Q 8   2♡–?   2NT–?   1♡–?
   ◊ J 9
   ♣ 9 7 4

Answers:

(a) Give partner a chance by raising to 3♡. If his opening is absolutely minimum this might be unfortunate, but there has been no interference bidding so there is a good chance that he will be able to go on to 4♡ and make it.

(b) Your's not to guess whether 3NT or 4♡ will be the better contract. Bid 3♡ (forcing, as it returns partner to his original suit after his 2NT rebid). He will know you have good, though not four-card heart support and will bid either 3NT or 4♡.

(c) Remember that a simple change-of-suit response after a previous pass is no longer forcing. With a near opener and a trump fit you can bid 2♠, not 1♠. 2♠ is a one-round force agreeing hearts as trumps, and opener must sign-off in 3♡ or, if strong enough, bid 4♡.

(Bids: 3♡, 3♡ and 2♠)

14 ♠ Q J 8 7 5 4   (a) 1♡–1♠   (b) 1♣–1♠   (c) 1♡–1♠
   ♡ 9 6 3   2♡–?   2♣–?   2◊–?
   ◊ K 8 4
   ♣ 6

Answers:

(a) The sooner you pass, the better. Opener has not bid strongly and you have no hopes of a game. He might make 2♡, though, if your singleton club and ◊ K fit in with his holdings.

(b) This time you have a singleton in partner's suit, not the useful three-card support you had in (a). Moreover your suit is a six-card major. Rebid 2♠, in itself a sign-off, which will yield a better score if you make it than 2♣ would do. If partner insists on playing in clubs now, he will know that he does so at his own peril!

(c) Though your diamond support is better in quality than your heart support, remember that partner may well be 5–4 in hearts and diamonds. Put him back to hearts as cheaply as possible.

(Bids: No Bid, 2♠ and 2♡)

15 ♠ K Q 10	(a) 1♠–2♡	(b) 1◊–1♡	(c) No
♡ K Q 8 6 5	3♡–?	2NT–?	1♠–?
◊ 10 7 3			
♣ J 9			

Answers:

(a) Show delayed support for spades with a rebid of 3♠. Partner will know that you lack the four-card support necessary for an immediate raise to 3♠, and also that you have not got delayed game raise values. Leave the choice of final contract to him.

(b) Raise to 3NT. Partner has shown 17–18 points, and though you have little in the minors, partner has bid diamonds and will surely have something in clubs which your ♣J will help to boost.

(c) This is virtually identical with the situation in 13 (c), the point of which was that, once having passed, a simple change-of-suit response is no longer forcing. So bid 3♡, showing a near opener and agreeing spades as trumps. Partner will know you lack four-card spade support, with which you would have bid 3♠, and he will either convert 3♡ to 3♠, which you would pass, or he will bid 4♠ direct.

(Bids: 3♠, 3NT and 3♡)

16 ♠ K Q J	(a) 1♠–2◊	(b) 1♡–2◊	(c) 1♣–1◊
♡ J 8 7 2	2NT–?	2NT–?	2NT–?
◊ A Q 9 8 3			
♣ 5			

Answers:

(a) Here again you meet the situation where, lacking four-card trump support, you wish to put the onus of deciding between 3NT and 4♠ onto your partner. This you do by making a forcing rebid of 3♠. He will know that you have adequate, though not four-card spade support, and the values for game somewhere.

(b) Being too strong for a first-round limit-bid of 3♡, your 2◊

was intended as the preliminary to a delayed game raise. No onus of any sort should be put on partner here – simply bid 4♡.

(c) As partner has now shown 17–18 points, you can rest assured that he has better than a three-card club suit (if you can't remember why, refer back to Section 1, 15). So in spite of your club singleton, raise to 3NT.

(Bids: 3♠, 4♡ and 3NT)

17 ♠ J 7 4   (a) 1♠–2♣ (b) 1♢–2♣ (c) 1♡–2♣
   ♡ Q 9 3   2♢–?   2NT–?   2♠–?
   ♢ 10 8
   ♣ A Q 7 6 3

Answers:

(a) Neither your count nor your stop in hearts is good enough for a rebid in no-trumps at this stage, and nor are you strong enough to suggest a game contract by the use of a fourth-suit-forcing bid as you did in 6(c). Just give quiet preference to 2♠ and leave it to partner who, after all, already knows you have 8 points.

(b) Partner has shown a count of 15–16 points, so between you you must have a minimum of 24, probably aided by your five-card suit. Raise to 3NT.

(c) Partner has made a forcing reverse, showing a strong hand with longer hearts than spades. As you *must* respond to this, you should give priority to showing a stop in the unbid suit if you can. With nothing in diamonds the sensible thing to do is to return partner to his first-bid suit by rebidding 3♡.

(Bids: 2♠, 3NT and 3♡)

18 ♠ K Q 10 6 (a) 1♡–1♠ (b) 1♢–1♠ (c) 1♠–2♣
   ♡ K J 9   2♡–?   2♢–3NT   2♠–?
   ♢ 7 6   4♢–?
   ♣ A J 7 3

Answers:

(a) Your first response was automatic, but when partner rebids 2♡ you know that he has at least a five-card suit. Raise to 4♡ which must be an odds-on bet facing your own 14 points.

(b) Any bid which removes an existing game contract to one

below game, as 4♢ does, is *forcing*. Clearly partner has long diamonds but 5♢ is a long way to go and you have the other three suits well held. Bid 4NT which, in view of your previous 3NT, followed by his take-out into 4♢, is not to be understood as Blackwood. Partner can pass or rescue himself into 5♢.

(c) 2♣ was a waiting bid on a hand too good for 3♠ which might be passed or for a direct 4♠ which might cost a good slam. Make the delayed game raise to 4♠.

(Bids: 4♡, 4NT and 4♠)

19	♠ K J 10 9	(a) 1♡–1♠	(b) 1♢–1♠	(c) No
	♡ Q 10 8	2♣–?	2NT–?	1♢–?
	♢ Q J 10 6			
	♣ 9 3			

Answers:

(a) The quality of your hand is rather good for a sign-off into 2♡, and nor do you want to give jump preference to 3♡ until you are sure opener's heart suit is rebiddable. Temporise with 2NT for which you are up to strength anyway.

(b) Even though partner has opened in a minor, a return to his original suit after his 2NT rebid is forcing. Bid 3♢ from which he will understand that you have good diamond support though you made the possibly more constructive bid of 1♠ first. He will also realise that you have a weak spot somewhere (clubs), and he must now decide between bidding 3NT or going on in diamonds.

(c) Once having passed originally, a 1♠ response would no longer be forcing though clearly this hand 'belongs' in diamonds. Bid an invitational 3♢, a limit-bid, but partner will convert to 3NT if he can.

(Bids: 2NT, 3♢ and 3♢)

20	♠ Q 9 3 2	(a) 1♡–3♡	(b) 2♡–4♡	(c) 2♣–2NT
	♡ K 7 4 3	4♢–?	4NT–?	3♢–?
	♢ K Q 6			
	♣ 8 4			

Answers:

(a) 4♢ is a cue-bid made in the light of your strong limit-bid of

3♡. You have no additional values and no first-round controls, so sign off in 4♡.

(b) Your direct raise to 4♡ promised in the region of 9–10 points with no first-round controls, i.e. *no* ace or void. In spite of this partner is interested in a possible slam and he is now asking about kings on the Blackwood scale. Bid 5♡ to show two.

(c) Your 2NT was positive, denying nothing but a reasonably biddable suit. Simply agree trumps by raising to 4◊. Had the rebid been 3♣ you would have rebid 3NT.

(Bids: 4♡, 5♡ and 4◊)

21   ♠ 8 3   (a) 1♣–1◊   (b) 1♡–3♡   (c) 1♠–2◊
     ♡ A J 8 7   1♡–?   3NT–?   3♣–?
     ◊ K 10 7 5 4
     ♣ Q 6

Answers:

(a) Partner may have only a four-card heart suit and be taking his opportunity to show this at the one-level. However, had he opened 1♡ you would have raised to 3♡, so do this now.

(b) It is virtually certain that partner has only a four-card suit, but with your two doubletons the idea of playing in no-trumps is not attractive to you. You will never know before the hand is played whether 3NT or 4♡ is better, but from your angle 4♡ looks the more promising, so bid it.

(c) 3♣, a new suit at the three-level, is forcing, but don't make the mistake of bidding 3♡, busily showing both red suits when partner has the black ones. Bid 3NT to show your heart stop.

(Bids: 3♡, 4♡ and 3NT)

22   ♠ A Q J 9 6   (a) 1♡–1♠   (b) 1◊–1♠   (c) 2♡–3♡
     ♡ K J 8   2♣–?   2♣–?   4NT–?
     ◊ Q 7
     ♣ 9 8 6

Answers:

(a) Bid a fourth-suit-forcing 2◊, asking for help in this department for a no-trump contract. Partner will give priority to a no-trump rebid, failing which he will choose the most expressive suit rebid, leaving you to decide the best final contract.

(b) Note the difference from (a) above, as this time you have an excellent guard in the fourth suit yourself. Bid 3NT, what your hand is worth.

(c) Note that trump agreement is more likely to help a partner who has opened with a strong two than a change-of-suit response. The single raise, unlike the direct raise to the four-level, promises *at least one* ace or void. 4NT is, therefore, the Blackwood request to show aces and you respond 5♢ to show one.

(Bids: 2♢, 3NT and 5♢)

23	♠ J 7	(a) 1♠–2♣	(b) 1♢–2♣	(c) 2♠–3♣
	♡ Q 8 2	2♡–?	4♣–?	3♡–?
	◊ K J 5			
	♣ A Q 9 8 5			

Answers:

(a) Show your values and good diamond stop by a rebid of 3NT. A raise to 3♡ might be passed and a direct raise to 4♡ might land you in a 4–3 fit.

(b) Partner has deliberately by-passed the 3NT level which means you are headed for a minor suit game or slam contract. Be as helpful as you can by bidding 4◊ to show diamond support.

(c) In a simple sequence such as (a) you rebid in no-trumps, but a partner with a two-suiter worth a strong two opening is not likely to be interested in a no-trump contract. Raise to 4♡ which is more likely to be helpful than a rebid of 3NT.

(Bids: 3NT, 4◊ and 4♡)

24	♠ A Q J 9	(a) 1♠–4♣	(b) 1◊–1♡	(c) 1♣–1♡
	♡ K 10 9 4	4NT–?	2◊–?	3◊–?
	◊ 7 2			
	♣ A 8 5			

Answers:

(a) Your Swiss 4♣ has already shown two aces, four-card trump support, and 13–15 points. Not asking a question to which he already knows the answer, therefore, partner is now enquiring about kings. Respond 5◊ on the Blackwood scale to show one.

(b) You had the values for a first-round response of 3NT, but rightly chose the possibly more constructive and less cramping bid of 1♠. Bid 3NT now, as you can't afford to be out of a game contract with 14 points facing an opening bid.

(c) In the light of partner's forcing rebid you are far too strong to rebid 3NT. Bid 4♣, by-passing the 3NT level. Compare this hand with 21 (c) where your initial response had already shown a minimum of 8 points.

(Bids: 5◊, 3NT and 4♣)

25 ♠ A K 6   (a) 1♣–1♡   (b) 1◊–1♡   (c) 1♣–1♡
    ♡ K Q 10 7 6   2♣–?   2♣–?   1♠–2◊
    ◊ 8 3   2NT–?
    ♣ J 9 3

Answers:

(a) The best rebid here is 2♠, a responder's reverse and a one-round force. It shows a good stop in the reverse-bid suit and though it might even show a second suit, it guarantees a good hand able to stand preference to the original suit at the three-level. Opener should give priority to a rebid in no-trumps if he can stop the fourth suit. Obviously opener must not give enthusiastic raises to the reverse-bid suit, but should treat it as exploration towards a no-trump contract.

(b) Bid a fourth-suit-forcing 2♠ to get opener to clarify his hand, after which you will be in a good position to judge the best final contract.

(c) Your fourth-suit-forcing 2◊ has been given confirmation that partner holds something in diamonds. Raise now to 3♠, telling him that 3NT was not necessarily your final goal, leaving him to choose between spades and no-trumps.

(Bids: 2♠, 2♠ and 3♠)

26 ♠ K J 7 2   (a) 1♡–1♠   (b) 2♠–4♠   (c) 2♣–2♠
    ♡ K J 6   2◊–?   5◊–?   2NT–?
    ◊ 8 4
    ♣ K 6 5 3

Answers:

(a) Your choice lies between a raise to 3♡ (not mere preference to 2♡) or a rebid of 2NT to show your count and club stop. The latter is the better choice.

(b) Partner is making a slam try which, as he knows you have no ace or void, must mean that he has at least three first-round controls himself. Respond by showing the cheapest second-round control you have, 5♡, which he will know is either the king or a singleton.

(c) You would – and did – bid 1♠ over 1♡, as in (a) and equally, with a hand worth a positive response to 2♣, you can show even a modest suit at the two-level. Now opener rebids 2NT showing 23–24 points. Raise direct to 6NT knowing you have a combined minimum count of 34 points.

(Bids: 2NT, 5♡ and 6NT)

27	♠ A K J 9 8	(a) 1♡–2♠	(b) 3♣–3♠	(c) 3♡–4◊
	♡ K J 9	2♡–3◊	4♠–?	4♡–?
	◊ A K J 10	3♡–?		
	♣ 4			

Answers:

(a) Partner has signed off as clearly as he can. Nevertheless you know about your heart fit, singleton club, and outside strength. You won't be bidding your hand twice if you now press on to 4NT, as with even one ace in his hand, 6♡ becomes a good proposition.

(b) Your change-of-suit response, even to a pre-emptive three-bid, is a one-round force. Made in a major suit, it shows a good suit which partner may raise on a doubleton-queen or three small. In view of his original 3♣ opening, settle for the game contract by passing.

(c) A change-of-suit response in a *minor* should be understood as a slam try, probably in the suit opened. In view of your heart fit you must now ask whether partner has even one ace, as you are willing to play in 5♡ if he has none.

(Bids: 4NT, No Bid and 4NT)

28	♠ K J 7	(a) 2◊–3NT	(b) 2♣–2NT	(c) 2◊–3NT
	♡ K J 4	4NT–?	3◊–?	4◊–?
	◊ 9 8 3			
	♣ Q 10 8 6			

Answers:

(a) 3NT shows 10–12 points, with no biddable suit. It would be senseless to regard partner's 4NT as quantative in this situation, so it must be a request for you to show aces. With none, of course, you respond 5♣ on the Blackwood scale.

(b) With 10 points you are too good for an initial 2♦ response, but partner's 3♦ rebid shows the one suit for which you have no active support. Rebid 3NT.

(c) Partner's 4♦, which removes an existing game contract to one below game level, is forcing. Just raise to 5♦ if that's the way he wants it – he already knows the sort of hand you have.

(Bids: 5♥, 3NT and 5♦)

29 ♠ Q972   (a) 1♠–2♠   (b) 2♠–3♠   (c) 4NT–5♥
    ♥ A J 3   3♣–?   4♣–?   5♠–?
    ♦ 76
    ♣ 9874

Answers:

(a) You can't confirm 'help' in clubs or a maximum 2♠ raise in response to partner's 3♣ trial bid. Compromise by making a 'passing the buck' bid of 3♥ showing where you have some values.

(b) Having guaranteed at least one ace or void by your 3♠ bid, partner is now angling to discover just what you have got. Unlike the 3♣ bid in (a), 4♣ is a cue-bid. Respond by a cue-bid of your own ace, 4♥.

(c) Many people forget that a 4NT opening does NOT call for Blackwood responses. With no ace you bid 5♣, with one ace you cue-bid the suit (6♣ for the ♣A) and with two aces bid 5NT. It is not for you to reason why he bid 4NT, but you have responded truthfully, after which you must pass any rebid he makes, as this will be his decision as to the final contract.

(Bids: 3♥, 4♥ and No Bid)

30 ♠ K J 6   (a) 1♣–1NT (b) 1♥–2NT (c) 1♣–1NT
    ♥ J 98   2NT–?   3♦–?   2♠–?
    ♦ Q98
    ♣ K952

Answers:

(a) Three easy ones to end with. First, having shown 8–10 points by bidding 1NT, your partner is now inviting 3NT. Having your full 10 point maximum, go to 3NT.

(b) A trifle under strength for your initial 2NT, which was the lesser evil than the possible alternatives, you are now faced with a forcing rebid. 5 ◊ seems a dangerous contract, so rebid 3NT.

(c) This is not a forcing reverse, as doubtless partner intended to rebid a simple 1 ♠ over a red suit response. He must, therefore, have a black two-suiter which he doesn't fancy for no-trumps and both must be at least five-card suits. Give him 3 ♠, confirming spade support and a maximum for your 1NT.

(Bids: 3NT, 3NT and 3 ♠)

Competition quiz

In competition against another player, each in turn should answer a full page of six questions. As an added exercise, you might like to decide on the correct first-round response before going on to the scoring questions on responder's rebids. You met all the original responses in Section 2 and now you are asked to name your next bid in each of the auctions shown.

1A	1	♠ K J 7 2	2	♠ K J 8 2	3	♠ K J 7 2
		♡ 9 8 6 5		♡ Q 10 7		♡ Q 10 8 3
		◊ 9 3		◊ 9 5		◊ J 8 6
		♣ Q J 10		♣ K Q J 3		♣ 10 8
		1 ◊ –1 ♠		1 ♡ –1 ♠		1 ♣ –1 ♡
		2 ♣ –?		2 ◊ –?		1 ♠ –?

Answers:

Bid		Reason
(2 points)		(3 points)
1	No Bid	Your hand is worth only one bid (unless you find yourself required to show preference by a rebid). Here show your preference for clubs by passing.
2	2NT	Show your club stop and 10–12 points with this limit-bid.

3   No   First check back to Section 2, 8, if you failed to get the
      Bid   correct first response here and on 1. In both these
            hands you had the values for only one forward-going
            bid and here, when partner's rebid comes in a suit for
            which you have an excellent fit, you pass.

What would you bid next on the same hands in these
sequences?

    4   1♡–2♡   5   1◊–1♠   6   1◊–1♡
       3◊–?   2NT–?   2♣–?

Answers:

Bid   Reason
(2 points)   (3 points)

4   3♡   3◊ is a trial bid and, therefore, a one-round force.
            Even with diamond 'help' your hand is too poor to do
            more than sign off.

5   3NT   Opener has shown 17–18 points which your hand
            more than adequately makes up to game values.

6   2◊   This is a simple preference bid and *not* a raise.

1B   1   ♠ K J 7 2   2   ♠ K J 6   3   ♠ J 9 8 6
          ♡ K 10 8 4   ♡ 9 6 5 3   ♡ Q 10 8 4
          ◊ A 6 2   ◊ A Q J 8 3   ◊ K 8
          ♣ 10 6   ♣ 7   ♣ 7 6 2

          1◊–1♡   1♠–2◊   1◊–1♡
          2♣–?   2♡–?   2♣–?

Answers:

Bid   Reason
(2 points)   (3 points)

1   2NT   Note the initial 1♡ bid, on a hand good enough for
            another bid if partner signs-off in 2◊. Now, with a
            good spade stop and 10–12 points, show your count.

2   4♡   Had partner opened 1♡ you would have used a
            delayed game raise sequence via 2◊ to ensure a 4♡
            contract. Now, when he rebids in hearts, you must
            show your full values and four-card fit by a jump to
            4♡.

3   No   Note the original 1♡ response on this weak hand with
     Bid two four-card majors. Show your club preference by
          passing.

What would you bid next on the same hands in these
sequences?

4 1♡–3♡	5 1♡–2◇	6 1♠–2♠
4♣–?	3♣–?	3◇–?

Answers:

Bid	Reason
(2 points)	(3 points)

4   4◇   4♣ is a cue-bid showing first-round control, which
          must mean that opener is making a slam try. Make a
          cost-nothing return cue-bid showing, not a diamond
          suit, but a control.

5   4♡   3♣, a new suit at the three-level, is forcing. Show your
          heart fit and strength by a jump to 4♡, not a mere
          3♡.

6   3♠   Even though partner makes a hopeful trial bid and
          you have 'help' for him in that department, your hand
          is too weak to do more than sign off by returning him
          to 3♠.

2A	1 ♠ K Q 9 3	2 ♠ K Q 10 9 7 3	3 ♠ Q 10 7
	♡ 10 7 4	♡ 8 4	♡ 5
	◇ A 6 4	◇ 7 5	◇ A Q J 8 4
	♣ K J 10	♣ J 6 4	♣ A Q J 6
	1♡–1♠	1♡–1♠	1♡–2◇
	2◇–?	2◇–?	2♡–?

Answers:

Bid	Reason
(2 points)	(3 points)

1   3NT Bid your own cards and don't wait for partner to bid
          them for you! With 14 points (two tens) and an
          excellent club stop the least you can do is go straight
          to 3NT.

2   2♠   Your own suit is good enough to rebid or put partner
            back to 2♡.
3   3♣   Your failure to force originally was due to lack of heart
            fit, but even when partner signs off you must press on
            in an attempt to find the best game contract. 3♣, a
            new suit at the three-level, is a one-round force and if
            partner can show some holding in spades with 3NT,
            you will be happy to pass.

What would you bid next on the same hands in these
sequences?

        4 1♡–1♠   5 1♡–1♠   6 1♡–2♢
           2♣–?   3NT–?   2♡–3♣
                                          4♢–?

Answers:

Bid   Reason
(2 points)   (3 points)

4   2♢   You feel sure that between you, you have game
            values, but are *not* sure as to the best final denomina-
            tion. Get partner to clarify his hand by bidding a
            fourth suit forcing 2♢. With as much as ♢Q–x he will
            rebid in no-trumps. If he bids 2NT you will raise to
            3NT which, with the lead coming up to his hand,
            should be the best bet.
5   4♠   This is likely to be much safer than 3NT.
6   5♢   Partner has denied even a partial spade guard so you
            would bid no-trumps at your peril! However, he is
            likely to have at least three-card diamond support, so
            go for 5♢.

2B   1 ♠ 7   2 ♠ J 9   3 ♠ 7 4
        ♡ Q 9 2   ♡ J 7 4   ♡ 9
        ◇ A Q J 8   ◇ A Q 10 9 3   ◇ A Q 10 9 7 6 4
        ♣ A J 10 9 3   ♣ K J 6   ♣ Q 6 2

        1♡–2♣   1♠–2♢   1♣–1♢
        2NT–?   2♡–?   2NT–?

Answers:

Bid	Reason
(2 points)	(3 points)

1   3♡   You are obviously nervous of a no-trump contract, but if opener has only a four-card heart suit . . . ? Bid a forcing 3♡, leaving the choice between 3NT and 4♡ to partner. He will know that he is not getting four-card heart support from you.

2   2NT   This, of course, promises a club guard – the unbid suit.

3   3NT   Partner doesn't like your diamonds, but you have 25–26 points between you, enough for a game try in no-trumps.

What would you bid next on the same hands in these sequences?

    4 1♠–2♣   5 1♣–1◇   6 1♡–2◇
       2♡–?   1♠–?   3♣–?

Answers:

Bid	Reason
(2 points)	(3 points)

4   3NT   You have an extremely good holding in diamonds, the unbid suit. Never mind your singleton – partner's bid this suit. Bid your full values, 3NT, not a mere 2NT.

5   2♡   A fourth-suit-forcing bid, asking partner to clarify his hand. With even a partial heart guard he will give priority to a rebid in no-trumps. 2♡ is forcing for one round, so if you don't like partner's answer the sequence can stop below game level.

6   3◇   3♣, a new suit at the three-level, is a one-round force asking *you* to clarify your hand. You can do nothing except repeat your diamonds.

3A 1	♠ J 10 7 4	2 ♠ A 8 6 3	3 ♠ J 9 2
	♡ A 10	♡ A 7 5	♡ A Q 3
	◇ A Q J 10 8 4	◇ 9 2	◇ A Q 10 7 4
	♣ 8	♣ K Q J 7	♣ Q 9
	1♣–1◇	1♣–1♠	1♠–2◇
	1♠–?	2♡–?	2♠–?

Answers:

Bid	Reason
(2 points)	(3 points)

1 4♠ Had partner opened 1♠ you would have taken definite steps to make sure at least a game contract was reached. He will not take a jump to 4♠ as a sign-off but as strength-showing.

2 3◇ A fourth-suit-forcing bid as you are not yet sure of the best possible game contract. 3◇ also promises one further bid if this is necessary to reach game so opener need not jump to game at this stage.

3 4♠ Once partner has rebid his spades, this should be the best final contract, particularly as you now know that he is not strong enough to bid any more forcefully.

What would you bid next on the same hands in these sequences?

4 1♠–4♣	5 1♠–4♣	6 1♠–2◇
4◇–?	4NT–?	2♡–?

Answers:

Bid	Reason
(2 points)	(3 points)

4 4♡ Your 4♣ was Swiss showing a trump fit, two aces, and 13–15 points, and the 4◇ rebid is a cue-bid – it is *not* showing a diamond suit! Cue-bid your own cheapest control.

5 5◇ Your 4♣ was Swiss showing a trump fit, two aces, and 13–15 points. As partner already knows you have two aces, he is asking for kings, and you show one on the Blackwood scale.

6   3♣   Mark time with a fourth-suit forcing bid to see wheth-
          er, in clarifying his hand, partner rebids one of his
          majors, after which you can put him to game in it.
          Remember you promise one further bid, so if he rebids
          3♡ or 3♠ you will raise.

3B   1 ♠ A 10 9 3   2 ♠ A J 10 7 4   3 ♠ K J 8
             ♡ Q 10 8   ♡ J 10 7 3   ♡ Q 10 8
             ◇ 7   ◇ 6   ◇ A J 9 7 6
             ♣ A K Q 6 3   ♣ A K 6   ♣ 7 6

             1♠–3♣   1◇–1♠   1♡–2◇
             3♠–?   2♣–?   2♠–?

Answers:

Bid   Reason
(2 points)   (3 points)

1   4♠   Don't fall into the temptation of bidding your hand
          twice by yourself pressing on for a slam. Opener
          knows you have the strength to force, and now he
          knows you can support spades, *he* may be able to go
          on.

2   3NT   With any luck partner has five in either minor and
          your ♣A–K should make this good for five tricks
          (surely four). You must have a guard in hearts and he
          has diamonds while you have spades. Don't bid 2NT
          on 13 points, when this might be passed.

3   4♡   Partner has reversed showing a strong hand with
          hearts longer than spades, which makes ♡Q–10–8
          very adequate support. 3♡ would be a mere prefer-
          ence, when you have the values for game.

What would you bid next on the same hands in these
sequences?

        4 1♡–3♣   5 1♡–4♣   6 1♠–2◇
           3♡–?   4NT–?   2♡–?

Answers:

Bid		Reason
(2 points)		(3 points)

4   4♡   As in 1 above, leave it to opener to decide whether to go on for a slam or not. He will have got the message that you have the strength to force, but you have not got much extra to this.

5   5◇   As in 4 on the previous page, your 4♣ was Swiss showing a trump fit, two aces, and 13–15 points. Partner now asks how many kings you have – show one.

6   3♠   A raise, as distinct from a preference, to partner's first bid suit. Compare 3 on the previous page where you yourself had a partial club stop, so were interested in a possible no-trump game contract.

4A

1 ♠ A 10 8 3	2 ♠ A 10 9 7 5	3 ♠ A J 10 6
♡ Q J 9 4	♡ Q 7 4	♡ K 10 9 4
◇ 7 6	◇ 6	◇ 7 2
♣ A 9 3	♣ A K 9 4	♣ K 6 3
1♡–4♣	1♡–1♠	1♣–1♡
4NT–?	2♡–?	2◇–?

Answers:

Bid		Reason
(2 points)		(3 points)

1   5♣   Your 4♣ was Swiss again, so as opener already knows you have two aces, he is asking if you have any kings. Respond 5♣ to show none – the Blackwood scale.

2   4♡   Once partner rebids his hearts you can raise direct to game. There is no need to investigate further.

3   3NT   Whether or not opener's minor suit reverse is forcing is one of those arguable points, though many expert players would take it as forcing. At least it must be very highly invitational. With the good spade holding, go to game in no-trumps, Note, by the way, the original heart response.

What would you bid next on the same hands in these sequences?

4 1◇–1♡	5 1♡–1♠	6 1♡–3♡
2♣–?	4♠–?	4◇–?

Answers:

Bid	Reason
(2 points)	(3 points)

4 2NT Again note the original heart response. Show your 10–12 points and spade stop with the 2NT limit-bid.

5 4NT Partner sounds as though he has 'reversing' values in hearts and spades. An immediate slam try is the only possible response – remember that 4♠ is not a shut-out but intended to make sure that at least a game contract is reached.

6 4♠ Partner must be angling for a slam contract as he is now making a cue-bid. You are maximum for your original 3♡ so make a return cue-bid of 4♠, even though this must drive the contract to at least 5♡. But almost for certain the ♠A is what opener is hoping you will have.

4B 1 ♠ K J 9 7 5	2 ♠ K Q 9 7 5	3 ♠ K Q 9 7 5
♡ K 9 8 4	♡ K J 10 9	♡ A 9
◇ J 6 3	◇ J 6 3	◇ J 6 3
♣ 8	♣ Q	♣ Q 7 2
1 ◇–1♠	1 ◇–1♠	1 ◇–1♠
2♣–?	2♣–?	2♣–?

Answers:

Bid	Reason
(2 points)	(3 points)

1 2◇ Compare these three hands carefully. In the first you are not strong enough to investigate a no-trump contract in spite of your heart stop, so just give preference to 2◇.

2 2NT Here you *don't* go bidding against your partner in the

majors while he bids the minors. Show your values and good – even biddable in different circumstances – heart suit with 2NT.

3   2♡   This time a genuine fourth-suit forcing bid of 2♡ will show interest in the best game contract – no-trumps if partner can help with hearts. So make sure you understand that a bid in the fourth suit, until developments of the auction show otherwise, *asks* about that suit but doesn't *show* it.

What would you bid next on the same hands in these sequences?

```
        4  1♣–1♠       5  1♡–1♠       6  1♡–1♠
           3NT–?          2◇–?           2♣–?
```

Answers:

Bid	Reason
(2 points)	(3 points)

4   No   Partner is showing 19 points and either your spade bid
      Bid   has done something to fill a gap or all he needed was to know you could respond, if only at the one-level. Pass and leave him to play.

5   4♡   You had a first-round choice of 1♠ or an immediate 4♡ (being too good for 3♡). Now give a delayed game rise to 4♡.

6   2◇   Once again fourth-suit-forcing comes to the rescue, not showing diamonds but asking about them, as if partner can help to 'boost' your ◇J into a stop, 3NT is likely to be the best game contract. But a two-level fourth-suit bid does not commit you to bid again if you don't like what you hear.

```
5A  1  ♠ 6 3 2        2  ♠ A K 9 7 5      3  ♠ J 9 8 6
       ♡ A J 10 6        ♡ A Q 8 6 3         ♡ K 6 2
       ◇ 7              ◇ J 7               ◇ J 10 4
       ♣ A K 7 5 4      ♣ 6                 ♣ A 7 5

       1♠–2♣            1◇–1♠               1♡–1♠
       2◇–?             2♣–?                2♣–?
```

Answers:

Bid	Reason
(2 points)	(3 points)

1   3NT   Don't bid against partner by showing clubs and hearts while he has spades and diamonds. 3NT should be the best contract.

2   2♡   You may think that, now you are familiar with fourth-suit-forcing, life is difficult for you here. Not a bit of it – remember the comment in **4B**, 3. Bid 2♡ and await the coming developments.

3   2♡   Simple preference to partner's first suit is all you can bid. If your four-card suit had been any other than one you could show at the one-level you would have bid 1NT in the first place.

What would you bid next on the same hands in these sequences?

    4   1♡–4♣   5   1◇–1♠   6   No
        4NT–?   2♣–2♡   1♣–?
                     2NT–?

Answers:

Bid	Reason
(2 points)	(3 points)

4   5◇   What a difference the 1♡ opening makes to the bidding of this hand! Now you have a first-round Swiss response. Show one king on the Blackwood scale in response to his 4NT.

5   4♡   Partner has, of course, taken your 2♡ as fourth-suit forcing and has replied showing at least a partial guard in the suit. This means a partial fit, perhaps ♡K–x or ♡J–x–x and as no one could expect you to want to play this two-suiter in no-trumps if a suit contract can be discovered, bid 4♡.

6   1NT   Having already passed it is better to show your count of 8–10 points than to bid 1♠, a suit in which you are not extremely anxious to be left to play, even at the one-level.

5B 1 ♠ K Q 9 8 6   2 ♠ Q 8   3 ♠ K J 10 6 4
           ♡ K J 9   ♡ 9 3   ♡ A 10
           ◇ J 10 5   ◇ 7 4   ◇ 6 2
           ♣ 7 4   ♣ A K Q J 10 8 5   ♣ A J 8 5

           1♡–1♠   1♡–2♣   1♡–1♠
           2NT–?   2◇–?   2◇–?

Answers:

Bid		Reason
(2 points)		(3 points)

1   3♡   In search of the best game contract, has partner got a four or five-card heart suit – will 4♡ be better than 3NT? Ask with a forcing 3♡ (a return to opener's suit after his 2NT rebid), which requires him to make the choice. He will not expect four-card heart support as you could not bid an immediate 3♡ in the first place.

2   2♠   5♣ is a long way to go and 3NT would be a pure 'shoot'. Ask partner if he can help with something in spades as well as his red suits, with a fourth-suit-forcing 2♠.

3   3NT No need to ask about anything here – just settle for 3NT which your hand is worth. You need no help to stop clubs.

What would you bid next on the same hands in these sequences?

       4 1◇–1♠   5 2♡–4♣   6 1♣–1♠
          2♣–?   4♡–?   2♠–?

Answers:

Bid	Reason
(2 points)	(3 points)

4   2NT Only 10½ points, but you must show the heart stop in this hand, which is certainly worth another forward-going move.

5   No   Your 4♣ was conventional, showing a solid and self-
    Bid supporting club suit, but partner is still not interested. He must know that two aces are missing or that he has

a likely heart loser as well as one missing ace. Trust his judgement.

6 **4♠** With a hand worth a 1♠ opening in the first place a spade game contract is the obvious one. As it doesn't look slam-worthy, just bid what you expect to make.

6A

1	♠ 9 4	2	♠ K 9 8 4	3	♠ K J 7
	♡ K J 8		♡ Q 6 3		♡ K 9 3 2
	◇ K J 7 2		◇ Q 10 9 2		◇ –
	♣ K 6 3 2		♣ 6 5		♣ Q J 9 7 6 2
	2♡–4♡		2♣–2◇		2♠–3♠
	4NT–?		2♠–?		4♣–?

Answers:

Bid	Reason
(2 points)	(3 points)

1 **5♠** Don't forget that by your jump to 4♡ you denied any first-round control; so partner already knows you are aceless, and he is asking for your kings on the Blackwood scale.

2 **4♠** Partner already knows you could do no better than an initial 2◇ response. The jump to 4♠ now shows scattered strength below positive requirements – which you have – no ace or void, and good trump support. This bid is, of course, a modified version of the direct raise to the four-level facing a strong two.

3 **4◇** Note the single raise in a hand which contains good trump support and a first-round control – the diamond void. When partner cue-bids the clubs (very possibly a void of his own), cue-bid your diamond void.

What would you bid next on the same hands in these sequences?

4	2♠–3NT	5	2♣–2◇	6	2♠–3♠
	4NT–?		3♣–?		4◇–?

Answers:

| Bid (2 points) | | Reason (3 points) |

4   5♣ The 3NT response to 2♠ conventionally shows about 10–11 points, and no biddable suit. 4NT here should be taken as Blackwood, for what other means has opener by which to go slamming if he wants to find out more about your hand?

5   3NT The suit rebid, even though in clubs, makes the sequence forcing to game. Neither of your four-card suits is worth suggesting as trumps and you can't support clubs, so bid 3NT.

6   4♠ This is a pity, because you now know that your diamond void is duplication of values as partner must be showing the ace. You have no other control to show, so sign-off in 4♠.

6B

1 ♠ Q976
  ♡ AQJ
  ◇ J109
  ♣ J108

2 ♠ KJ976
  ♡ 84
  ◇ AJ2
  ♣ J108

3 ♠ K63
  ♡ 84
  ◇ KJ976
  ♣ J108

2♠–3♠
4♣–4♡
4♠–?

2♡–2♠
3◇–?

2♡–2NT
3♣–?

Answers:

| Bid (2 points) | | Reason (3 points) |

1   No   Your 3♠ showed at least one ace or void, not one only,
    Bid 4♣ was a cue-bid to which you respond by showing your lowest-ranking control, so you have *denied* control of diamonds. Trust partner's judgement when he signs off.

2   4◇ Your first response was positive, showing a suit and no reasonable heart support. Partner has now shown a second red suit and the least you can do is tell him that you like his second offer.

3   3◇ With only a negative response on the first round, you

are not particularly interested in either of partner's suits though you have too much not to try to help him into a game contract. Show your biddable suit.

What would you bid next on the same hands in these sequences?

4 2♣–2NT	5 2♣–2♠	6 2♠–2NT
3♠–?	2NT–?	3♣–?

Answers:

Bid	Reason
(2 points)	(3 points)

4 4♠ Don't hurry it – you've already made a positive response. Now just show that you like his suit and leave it to him – he can't fail to go 'slamming'.

5 6NT Partner is showing 23–24 points, as he would be doing by a 2NT rebid after 2♦ from you. You have a five-card suit as well as the points to bring your combined hands into the small slam range, so bid it.

6 4♠ Your hand was too modest to give an initial positive response, but you would be understanding it badly if you gave a mere preference bid of 3♠ now. ♠K–x–x is adequate support, and partner already knows you haven't got much.

Section 6

Contested Auctions

The basic rules

It is clearly beyond the scope of this book to attempt to cover all competitive situations, but the following details will give the student some guiding principles on which to base his bidding in many of the more usual situations. Emphasis is given to the possible difference an enemy opening or intervening bid can make.

1 *Immediate overcalls:*

W	N	E	S	
		1♡	1♠	At the one-level, and particularly when not vulnerable, an overcall need not be very strong. Even if doubled and left to play, a one-level contract takes a lot of defeating to make it a worthwhile exchange for a declarer score. For a one-level intervention you should be able to estimate four playing tricks if not vulnerable, or five if vulnerable. A five-card suit.
		1♡	2♢	At the two-level, playing strength is of great importance, and unless a six-card suit is held there should be adequate compensating honour

W	N	E	S	
				strength. You should be able to estimate five playing tricks if not vulnerable and six if vulnerable.
		1♡	1NT	An intervening 1NT is strong, the barest minimum being 15 points preferably including a double stop in the enemy's suit.
		1♡	Dbl	This is a request to partner to take out into his own best suit. Should be used on hands on which it seems wiser to discuss the final trump suit with partner rather than tell him your own good suit. Partner's responses are set out in 6 on pp. 196–7.
		1♡	2♠	Next in strength, on a 'shape' hand, comes a jump in a new suit. This shows a good playable suit of at least six-card length, in a hand too good for a simple overcall at the lowest available level. It is highly invitational but not forcing.
		or		
		1♠	3♣	
		1♡	2♡	An immediate cue-bid of the suit opened shows a 'shape' hand even stronger than the jump overcall. It is a game force and may be used on a strong single or two-suited hand. Knowing the strength facing him, partner will keep open to game showing four-card suits in ascending order.

2 *Re-opening in the protective position:*

W	N	E	S	
1♡	–	–	1♠	Fourth-in-hand after two passes,

W	N	E	S	
				South should re-open the bidding competitively if possible, as once opener's partner has passed (and is, therefore, known to be extremely weak) there is a good chance that North has a share of the outstanding values even though he could not intervene immediately – possibly because of a good holding in the suit opened. The weakest protective bid, a change-of-suit at the one-level, can be made on as little as 8 or 9 points and a biddable suit.
1♡	–	–	2◇	A protective bid at the two-level shows at least a five-card suit and better than 8 or 9 points.
1♡	–	–	2♠	A jump bid in a new suit shows a good hand with a good playable suit and a wish to contest for a part-score or even possibly a game.
1♠	–	–	1NT	This shows 11–15 points and a stop in the suit opened. Note the difference from an immediate 1NT overcall.
1◇	–	–	Dbl	Shows 9 or more with tolerance for any suit into which partner may take out or on which South would not be dismayed to defend if North converts to a business double by passing.
1♠	–	–	2♠	A cue-bid of the suit opened is forcing to suit agreement, which means that it may be used on rela-

W	N	E	S

tively weak hands of suitable shape (4–4–4–1 with a singleton in the suite opened is ideal), as the bidding can be dropped below game once a suit fit has been discovered. If the cue-bidder's hand is strong, therefore, it is up to him to bid on. A player responding to a 'protective' bid must remember the low values which may be held by partner and respond accordingly.

3 *Responding to a suit intervening bid:*

W	N	E	S
1♡	1♠	–	2◇
1♡	2◇	–	3◇

A simple change-of-suit response to partner's intervening bid is *not* forcing, for which reason South should give priority to a raise of North's bid suit if this is possible, leaving a change-of-suit bid as a denial of support for North's suit. Other bids in South's position are largely a matter of common sense, but see 7 on p. 197.

4 *Responding after an intervening bid:*

W	N	E	S
	1♠	2◇	2♠
			or 3♠

Suit limit-bids are unaffected by an intervening bid, and should be given to the full values held.

W	N	E	S
	1♠	2◇	2NT
			or Dbl

In the case of no-trump limit-bids in response, the same values as in an uninterrupted sequence are shown but a good stop in the suit intervened is also guaranteed. A business double is probably better.

W	N	E	S
	1♠	–	2♣

A suit intervention by East may obstruct South's change-of-suit response if he is good enough to bid at the two-level but not at the three-level. It may then be necessary for him to find a substitute response such as a suit raise on less than four-card support.

W	N	E	S
	But		
	1♠	2♡	2♠

W	N	E	S
	1♡	1♠	Dbl

A double of a suit intervention is for business, by inference showing lack of support for opener's suit.

W	N	E	S
	1♡	1NT	?

Responses after a 1NT intervention (a strong bid) are natural and based on common sense. Generally, if North can open and East has at least 15 points for a no-trump bid, there's not much left for South!

5 *Bidding over opponent's take-out double:*

W	N	E	S
	1♡	Dbl	1♠

A simple take-out into a new suit is a rescue bid (non-forcing) showing a long – probably six-card – suit and a lack of fit for opener's suit.

W	N	E	S
	1♢	Dbl	1NT

Shows 7–8 points and may be used as an alternative to a pass, in the hope of making West's bid difficult.

W	N	E	S
	1♠	Dbl	Re-dbl

Shows a minimum of 9 points, no particular fit for partner's suit, and a probable interest in doubling the

W	N	E	S	
				opponent's final contract. It guarantees the ability to make one further bid. Opener should rebid on a hand quite unfitted for defence, but otherwise pass to give South the chance for which he has asked.
	1♢	Dbl	2♠	A jump bid in a new suit is pre-emptive showing a long suit but few points.
	1♠	Dbl	2♠ or 3♠	The limit-bids, when used after a take-out double, are geared down in value for their pre-emptive effect.
	1♡	Dbl	2NT	A responding hand containing full values for a limit raise to the three-level (in any suit, major or minor) is shown by a conventional bid of 2NT which opener should treat as he would a normal suit limit-bid of three.

6 *Responding to partner's take-out double:*

W	N	E	S	
1♠	Dbl	2♢	2♡	A bid by East lets South off the hook of replying to North's double and any bid he makes, therefore, becomes positive. As North is asking for South's best suit, South should always try to show a five-card suit, even on a weak hand, if he can do so at an economical level.
1♡	Dbl	–	1♠	
1♢	Dbl	–	1♠	
1♡	Dbl	–	1NT	Failing any action other than a pass by East, South should show his best suit, BUT a Herbert negative, i.e. a bid of the next higher-ranking suit may be used to show a 'bust',

W	N	E	S	
				any other bid showing at least a biddable suit. South should show a four-card major in preference to a five-card minor if the former does not involve the negative bid. South shows a better-than-minimum hand with some hold on the suit opened.
1◇	Dbl	–	2♡	A jump response shows a good playable suit, invitational but not forcing.
1♡	Dbl	–	–	Obviously shows strength in the enemy suit and the expectation that defending the doubled contract will yield the best result.
1♣	Dbl	–	2♣	If in doubt as to the best final denomination, a cue-bid of the suit opened passes the buck back to North to choose the suit. This is forcing to suit agreement, so on a strong hand it would be up to either member of the partnership to see that a game contract is reached.
1◇	Dbl	–	2NT	This is a common sense bid showing a good hand with a sure hold on the suit opened.

7 Directional asking bids:

N	E	S	W	
1◇	1♠	2♣	–	This is a bid in the opponent's suit, which may be used by either member of the partnership when no forcing situation exists, with a view to investigating for the best game
2♠				
1♡	–	2♣	2◇	
3♣	–	3◇		

N	E	S	W
1♡	1♠	2♠	–
1♡	1♠	2♠	–
2NT	–	3♡	–

contract, the accent being on the fact that this may well be 3NT. In each of these sequences the last bid is a DAB. It asks partner to clarify his hand, giving priority to a rebid in no-trumps at either the two or three-level according to strength or situation, if his hand contains a partial guard in the enemy's suit, which will boost the DAB bidder's own holding in the suit into at least one stop. An immediate overcall in the suit opened may be either a DAB or a strong bid inferentially agreeing partner's suit as trumps. Opener should give priority to a rebid in no-trumps at either the two- or three-level, according to his values. If South removes into North's original suit at his next turn, it becomes clear that a no-trump contract was not his final aim, and that he was making a forcing bid with a suit fit for opener and control of the enemy's suit.

8 *Unusual no-trump:*

W	N	E	S
1♠	No	2♢	2NT
1♡	–	–	2NT
1♡	–	1♠	–
3♣	–	4♡	4NT

Any bid in no-trumps which is clearly neither natural nor Blackwood requests partner to take action with a view to a probable sacrifice contract. If two suits have been bid by the opponents, it requests partner's choice between the remaining two. If only one major has been bid, it requests his choice between the minors.

Exercises

In this final section you can expect your opponents to enter the auction, either opening before your side has a chance to bid, or intervening; though in a few cases an uninterrupted sequence will also be shown to underline the difference this may make to the correct bid.

It would not be possible to cover the entire range of competitive situations in thirty examples, but at least these should give you an idea of how to cope with opposition bidding. In each case, you are South and must find your bid in the sequence shown.

1 Love All, dealer East:

♠ K 4 3
♡ A 6 3
◇ Q 9 5 4
♣ A 8 5

E	S	W	N		E	S	W	N
(a) No	?				(b) 1♡	?		

Answers:

(a) If using a weak no-trump, open 1NT, but if that is impossible because of the range you are using, you will have to fall back on a prepared 1♣.

(b) As an overcaller your hand is not strong enough for any competitive action. Pass and await developments – if any.

(Bids: 1NT or 1♣ and No Bid)

2 Game All, dealer East:

♠ A 9 4
♡ K J 6 5 3 2
◇ 7
♣ 6 3 2

E	S	W	N		E	S	W	N
(a) No	?				(b) 1◇	?		

Answers:

(a) This hand, particularly being vulnerable, is not even worth an Acol light opener, so pass initially.

(b) Now you have a sensible intervening overcall, particularly as this can be made at the one-level, which needs an awful lot of defeating if the opponents are to gain a worthwhile penalty.

When you are considering making an intervening call, playing tricks are of great importance. Notice, therefore, that some hands can be worth an opening bid but not an intervening bid, whilst others can be worth an intervention but not an opening.

(Bids: No Bid and 1♡)

3
♠ 10 9
♡ K J 3
◇ A Q 9 8 5
♣ J 10 8

Game All, dealer North:

	N	E	S	W		N	E	S	W
(a)	No	1♠	?		(b)	No	1◇	?	
(c)	1♠	2◇	?						

Answers:

(a) Being vulnerable, and particularly when partner has shown he has not got the values for an opening bid, this would be a very dangerous hand for intervention. Pass – you can always come in later if expedient.

(b) A double would be for a take-out – the last thing you want. Pass and await developments.

(c) Double! A perfect example of the reason why it is dangerous to make an intervening overcall without adequate playing strength.

(Bids: No Bid, No Bid and Double)

4
♠ Q 10 7
♡ A J 10 6
◇ 9 6 3
♣ J 9 5

Love All, dealer West:

	W	N	E	S		W	N	E	S
(a)	1◇	No	No	?	(b)	No	1♠	2◇	?

Answers:

(a) Once opener's partner, East, has passed, he is known to be woefully weak, which means that there is a reasonable chance that North holds a share of the remaining goodies – perhaps a hand such as 1, as he could not intervene. It is, therefore, up to a player in South's position to 'protect' his partner's pass, which he may do on much lesser values than he needs in the immediate overcalling position. The weakest and, therefore, least encouraging protective bid is a change-of-suit at the one level, so here South should re-open with 1♡.

(b) Without the intervening bid South would doubtless bid

1NT, but he can't show a diamond guard, let alone bid at the two-level. Nor, in all decency, can he pass and the best thing he can do, even without four-card spade support, is to give partner 2♠.

(Bids: 1♡ and 2♠)

5	Game All, dealer East:								
♠ K 10 8 6		E	S	W	N		E	S	W	N
♡ A Q 9 6 3	(a)	1◇	?			(b)	1NT*?			
◇ A 7 2							*12–14 points			
♣ 4										

Answers:

(a) You have no way of guessing whether North has a biddable major or possibly a string of clubs. *Ask* him by making a take-out double. If he bids 2♣ you can then take out into 2♡ but he will show a major suit if he can, knowing that your double implies willingness to play in either. (But compare 21, 22 and 23, which you will come to later.)

(b) You must have some method of defence against that damaging weapon, the weak no-trump, and one of the best is Astro. Here you would bid an Astro 2◇, which shows nine cards between spades and one of the other suits. The convention can be used against any strength of no-trump opening though, of course, allowance must be made if the opening 1NT is of the strong variety.

(Bids: Double and 2◇)

6	Love All, dealer West:								
♠ A Q 10 9 6 2		W	N	E	S		W	N	E	S
♡ K J 8	(a)	No	No	1◇	?	(b)	1◇	No	No	?
◇ A 8 4										
♣ 6										

Answers:

(a) This is a good strong single-suited hand too strong for a simple overcall (cf. 2 (b)). Bid 2♠, strong and highly invitational but not forcing. It will, however, tell North that you have a hand on which you'd like to go places but want to play in spades.

(b) Now in the protective position you are again much too strong for a mere 1♠ bid (cf. 4 (a)) – an Acol player never tells his partner he has one sort of hand when he has, in fact, another! Bid 2♠ which will encourage North to take action to help you if he can.

(Bids: 2♠ in both cases)

7   Game All, dealer North:

♠ Q 9 3   N   E   S   W   N   E   S   W
♡ K 10 6 4   (a) 1♠ No ?   (b) 1♡ 2◊ ?
◊ 8
♣ K 10 7 5 2   (c) 1♠ 2◊ ?

Answers:

(a) There is no competitive situation and, therefore, nothing to interfere with South's natural response of 2♣.

(b) An intervening bid makes no difference at all if a responding hand can still make a natural suit limit-bid. Here, without East's 2◊, South would bid 3♡, and he should do so now.

(c) When East's 2◊ bid deprives South of the two-level for the response he made in (a), it is out of the question for him to show his clubs at the three-level, and nor can he bid 2NT which would show 10–12 points *and* a stop in diamonds. The only sensible alternative is to raise 1♠ to 2♠, even without four-card support.

(Bids: 2♣, 3♡ and 2♠)

8   Game to N–S, dealer West:

♠ K J 10 5   W   N   E   S   W   N   E   S
♡ A 10 9 6   (a) No No 1◊ ?   (b) 1◊ No No ?
◊ A 8
♣ J 10 6

Answers:

(a) Another hand on which you can't allow 1◊ to go uncontested, yet would prefer to *ask* your partner rather than *tell* him which suit would fit his hand best for trumps, which you do by making a take-out double. Note that partner may decide to convert this to a business double by passing, for which reason you should not double on a hand which would be disastrous for defence.

(b) In the protective position the situation is different. Partner may have passed on a hand something like 3 and be longing for a chance to defend! A double in the protective position shows a minimum of 12 points with tolerance for any suit into which partner may take out *and* a hand which you would not fear to use in defence if North decides to pass. It's the correct bid here.

(Bids: Double in both cases)

9
♠ K J 10 3
♡ A Q
◇ K 10 9
♣ K J 9 4

Game All, dealer West:

W	N	E	S		W	N	E	S
(a) No	No	1♡	?	(b) 1♡	No	No	?

Answers:

(a) Irrespective of the agreed value of your opening no-trump, in Acol an intervening 1NT is *always strong* – a minimum of a good 15 points including at least two sure stops in the suit opened. Here, therefore, 1NT is the perfect bid. Partner should treat it as he would a strong no-trump opening, except that 2♣ would be a weak take-out and not a fit-finding bid.

(b) 1NT in the protective position shows 11–15 points and a stop in the suit opened. Clearly South can't tell his partner that *all* he has is 11–15 points, and a double would do less than justice to this hand. The answer is to cue-bid the suit opened, asking partner to show his own best suit. This is forcing to suit agreement which means that once a suit fit has been discovered the auction can be dropped. This in turn means that the bid can be used on quite a modest hand if of suitable shape, but that it is up to both North and South to bid up if it appears that game strength may be held.

(Bids: 1NT and 2♡)

10
♠ A K Q 9 7 4 2
♡ K 6
◇ A
♣ K Q 7

Game to E–W, dealer East:

E	S	W	N		E	S	W	N
(a) 1♡	?			(b) 1NT*?			
				*12–14 points			

Answers:

(a) You can't risk doubling for a take-out and a bid of 2♠ (cf. 6) would not do justice to this hand. Cue-bid the suit opened against you, i.e. bid 2♡, to which partner should respond as to a take-out double. You can then bid *and rebid* spades, to show the single-suited character of your hand.

(b) Double, which you hope and expect partner will pass for penalties. Many players, on most occasions successfully, use a weak no-trump at any score, but this is going to be a moment when East will wish he hadn't! His opening bid is pretty certain to contain the two missing aces so the best you could gain as declarer would be a non-vulnerable game and the penalty is going to be a good deal more valuable.

(Bids: 2♡ and Double)

11   Love All, dealer North:
♠ Q J 9 8 5 3
♡ 6 3 2   N   E   S   W   N   E   S   W
◇ 10 8   (a) 1◇ No ?   (b) 1◇ Dbl ?
♣ 8 3

Answers:

(a) There is always a temptation to show a six-card suit, particularly if it is a major, but any change-of-suit response is a one-round force, and you have not got enough to show North the values for a bid. Pass and await developments – you can always come in later, if expedient.

(b) A change-of-suit response after a take-out double is *no longer forcing*. Indeed it is a rescue operation showing a five or six-card suit which you think likely to be a better proposition than the suit partner has bid, so here you can bid 1♠. It won't deceive North, who will know that you have excellent alternative ways of showing different types of hands.

(Bids: No Bid and 1♠)

12   Love All, dealer North:
♠ 9 3
♡ A J 9 4   N   E   S   W   N   E   S   W
◇ K J 7   (a) 1♠ 2◇ ?   (b) 1♡ 2◇ ?
♣ Q 10 8 5   (c) 1♠ Dbl ?

Answers:

(a) The obvious bid is 2NT, showing the 10–12 points it would show without the intervening bid but, in this case, confirming the diamond guard as well.

(b) The intervening bid makes no difference at all on occasions when the responding hand is suitable for a suit limit-bid. Without the 2♢ bid you would respond 3♡ — do the same now.

(c) It can make a vast difference when the intervention is a take-out double. In this case, without much in partner's suit, the correct bid is a redouble. The message of this is that the hand contains a minimum of 9 points. It also guarantees the ability to make a further bid which will very likely be to double the enemy's final contract. For this reason North, unless he has an obviously more sensible course of action, should pass at his next turn to give South the chance he has asked for.

(Bids: 2NT, 3♡ and Redouble)

13   Love All, dealer North:
♠ Q 10 9   N   E   S   W   N   E   S   W
♡ A 9 5 2   (a) 1♣ 1♡ ?   (b) 1♣ Dbl ?
♢ J 7 6
♣ J 8 5

Answers:

(a) A response of 1NT when the opening bid has been 1♣ shows 8–10 points, and when there has been a suit intervening bid it also, of course, shows a guard in that suit. This hand meets these requirements, so 1NT let it be.

(b) Although the correct bid in this case is also 1NT, it is for quite a different reason. You will remember that a change-of-suit (cf. 11) is a rescue bid and redouble (cf. 12) shows a minimum of 9 points, so neither bid can be used here. 1NT after a take-out double shows a minimum of 7 points though not enough for a redouble. Your possible alternative of a pass will not interfere in any way with West's reply to the double, which 1NT may do.

(Bids: 1NT in both cases)

14   Love All, dealer North:
♠ K Q J 9 8 6   N   E   S   W   N   E   S   W
♡ 9 5   (a) 1◇ 1♡ ?   (b) 1◇ Dbl ?
◇ 8 7 4
♣ A 5

Answers:

(a) The obvious bid is the one-round force of 1♠. This is so elementary that you will realise it has only been included to emphasise the difference when East, instead of passing or bidding a suit, doubles.

(b) Your hand is far too good for a rescue bid of 1♠ (cf. 11) which would actually be asking North to pass. Nor can you redouble which, as you know, implies willingness to defend, for which your holding is quite unsuitable in spite of its count.

Make a jump bid of 2♠ which, in this situation, is a one-round force, not a game force. It will tell North of the single-suited character of your hand, which should leave him in a good position to judge whether to go on for a game or not.

(Bids: 1♠ and 2♠)

15   Game to E–W, dealer North:
♠ 9 5 3   N   E   S   W   N   E   S   W
♡ Q 10 7 4   (a) 1♡ No ?   (b) 1♡ Dbl ?
◇ Q 8 4
♣ 10 9 8

Answers:

(a) Whether or not East makes a bid you haven't enough to show support for partner, so pass. The best you can say about your hand is that at least it contains four-card heart support!

(b) Once more the double makes a difference, and this time you should raise to 2♡. You will realise that this ranks as a limit-bid, but that the limit is very much lower than in an uninterrupted sequence. The idea, of course, is to make things as difficult as possible for West, who has not yet had a chance to reply to his partner's question about his best suit.

(Bids: No Bid and 2♡)

16　　　　　　　　Game All, dealer North:

♠ K J 2　　　　　　　N　E　S　W　　　　N　E　S　W
♡ J 10 8 5 4　　　　(a) 1♡　No　?　　　(b) 1♡　Dbl　?
◇ 9 6 2
♣ 8 5

Answers:

(a) Vulnerable particularly, you haven't enough 'shape' to do more than give a single raise to 2♡ on this hand.

(b) The double again makes a difference and here, on the same principle that made you give a single raise on 15 with less than the standard requirements for the bid, you should bid 3♡. This will have the maximum possible pre-emptive effect on West, who has yet to bid. He *may* be able to bid 3♠, but either minor will have to be shown at the four-level. In any case, with the double on your right, your ♠K–J are likely to be well placed.

(Bids: 2♡ and 3♡)

17　　　　　　　　Game All, dealer North:

♠ 10 9　　　　　　　N　E　S　W　　　　N　E　S　W
♡ K 10 7 4　　　　(a) 1♡　No　?　　　(b) 1♡　Dbl　?
◇ A 8 4 2
♣ K 6 4

Answers:

(a) It wouldn't matter whether East passed or made a suit intervening bid here, as this makes no difference to your response when you have a suit limit-bid available. The correct and accurate bid here is 3♡.

(b) You have already learned (16) that, following a take-out double, a raise to the three-level is used purely pre-emptively, from which it follows that, in this situation, another bid must be found when a responding hand contains a genuine three-level limit-bid. The answer is to use a *conventional* bid of 2NT (an otherwise idle bid, as these values would be shown by a redouble) which shows the full values for a normal limit-bid at the three-level. North will treat this as he would the 3♡ bid in (a) above, simply signing-off by converting to 3♡, bidding 4♡ if he

would have done so in reply to 3♡, or taking any stronger action
he thinks justified.

(Bids: 3♡ and 2NT)

18   Game All, dealer South:
♠ A J 10 9 7   S   W   N   E   S   W   N   E
♡ 9 5   (a) 1♣   Dbl Re- 1◊   (b) 1♣   Dbl Re- No
◊ 7   dbl   dbl
♣ K Q 10 8 2   ?   ?

Answers:

(a) As long as you fully understand what North means when
he bids over West's take-out double, you won't find much
difficulty in adjusting your own rebids accordingly. In this
sequence North has shown a minimum of 9 honour points and a
probable willingness to double and then defend the opponents'
final contract. The last thing you want to do on this weak two-
suiter is to defend, so warn North of this immediately by
rebidding 1♠ instead of allowing the bidding to run round to
him for action.

(b) This makes no difference to the fact that you don't want to
defend. North's redouble let East off the hook of replying to his
partner's double but it doesn't change your view. Tell North this
by bidding 1♠.

(Bids: 1♠ in either case)

19   Game All, dealer South:
♠ 9 5 3   S   W   N   E   S   W   N   E
♡ A K J 10 9 4 (a) 1♡ Dbl 1♠   No   (b) 1♡   Dbl Re- 2◊
◊ 7 6   dbl
♣ K 10   ?   ?

Answers:

(a) Check back to 11 if you've forgotten the type of hand your
partner, North, is likely to have. Pass and leave it to him – he's
lucky to be finding three spades in your hand if he becomes
declarer.

(b) This is essentially the same situation as in 18 – you have no interest in defence even if North has the values for a redouble. Tell him this by taking out into 2♡.

(Bids: No Bid and 2♡)

20   Game All, dealer South:

♠ A 10 9

♡ K J 10 7

◇ K J 10

♣ A J 9

S	W	N	E		S	W	N	E
(a) 1♡	Dbl	1♠	No	(b)	1♡	Dbl	Re-dbl	No
?					?			

Answers:

(a) Without West's double, North's 1♠ would have been a one-round force to which you would have rebid 2NT. Now, however, that you know he is making a weak rescue-bid, it would be foolish indeed to go to this high level. Bid 1NT which North, in turn, should recognise as showing the values for a 2NT bid in an uninterrupted sequence. If North takes out into 2♠, you will pass.

(b) You are only too happy to allow North to take the next action, and if this is to double any get-out attempt by West, it will suit you excellently to defend. With 17 honour points in your hand and North's minimum of 9 points you have a combined total of at least 26 points, which must unstitch the vulnerable East–West in no uncertain terms. So pass and await developments.

(Bids: 1NT and No Bid)

21   Game All, dealer West:

♠ 8 6 3

♡ Q 10 9 4

◇ 8 5 4

♣ 9 3 2

W	N	E	S		W	N	E	S
(a) 1♣	Dbl	No	?	(b)	1♡	Dbl	No	?

Answers:

(a) On very weak hands such as this, where the bidding level must be kept as low as possible, many players find it convenient to use some sort of negative or 'bust' response. Recently I have been using a Herbert negative, that is, a bid of the next higher ranking suit to show not even a four-card suit which can be bid at the one-level. This has proved very satisfactory and, using it, you would bid 1 ♡ here. North will know that it is at least a four-card suit because you did not use the 'bust' response of 1 ◊.

(b) This time it is your only four-card suit which has been doubled, so you respond 1♠.

An important point to remember is that if East bids over the double, this lets South off the hook of responding and any bid he makes is, therefore, positive, showing at least a four-card suit. But South should always try to help his partner by showing his best suit as long as this can be at the one-level so in (a), had East bid 1 ◊, South should still bid 1 ♡, but had East bid 1 ♡ or 1♠, South should pass.

(Bids: 1 ♡ and 1♠)

22
♠ 10 3
♡ Q J 10 9 4 3
◊ 7 6
♣ K 9 2

Game All, dealer West:

W	N	E	S		W	N	E	S
(a) 1♣	Dbl	1 ◊	?	(b) 1♠	Dbl	No	?

Answers:

(a) Whether East bids his 1 ◊ or not, the answer would be the same here – South must make it clear to North that he is not showing a hand such as 21 above. Make a jump bid of 2♡, showing a genuinely playable suit.

(b) It would be cramping the auction to jump to 3♡ here so bid 2♡. But North will know that you did not use the negative bid of 2♣ and that you did not fear to raise the level of the bidding to show your suit.

(Bids: 2♡ in either case)

23
♠ J 9 7 6
♡ Q 10 8 4
◊ 9 5 4
♣ K 7

Game All, dealer West:

W	N	E	S		W	N	E	S
(a) 1 ◊	Dbl	No	?	(b) 1 ♡	Dbl	No	?

Answers:

(a) If you are using a Herbert negative you are prevented from using your simplest answer of 1 ♡ but, as almost always happens, your hand contains an alternative, in this instance 1♠.

North will notice that you did not use a negative response, even if 1♠ isn't very encouraging!

(b) This time the 'bust' response would be 1♠, which you would like to avoid, but you have no sensible alternative.

(Bids: 1♠ in either case)

24

♠ K 10 9 8
♡ A J 9 3
◇ 9 5 4
♣ K 8

Game All, dealer West:

W	N	E	S		W	N	E	S
(a) 1♣	Dbl	No	?	(b)	1♡	Dbl	No	?

Answers:

(a) On a promising hand, and particularly when you are doubtful as to the best final denomination, cue-bid the suit opened against you, so here bid 2♣. This bid is what is known as forcing to suit agreement – in other words, the bidding can be dropped below game-level once the best suit fit has been discovered, so it is up to either of the partnership to bid strongly if he thinks a game contract should be reached. This cue-bid is, of course, a 'passing the buck' bid, and if North next bids 2◇ South should pass. If North bids either 2♡ or 2♠, South should raise to three and leave the rest to North.

(b) When 1♡ is doubled a cue-bid of 2♡ would not be sensible. Nor would an apparent negative of 1♠ or a jump to 2♠ on a four-card suit. Bid 2NT showing the excellent count and hold on the enemy suit.

(Bids: 2♣ and 2NT)

25

♠ K J 7
♡ Q 5
◇ A K 10 9 8
♣ A J 8

Game to E–W, dealer South:

S	W	N	E		S	W	N	E
(a) 1◇	No	1♡	1♠	(b)	1◇	No	2♣	2♡
?					?			

Answers:

(a) With 18 points and an excellent guard in the suit bid on your right you have no problems. Bid the obvious 2NT. This question was only included to pinpoint the difference arising when, though you suspect that a final no-trump contract would be the best, your own stop in the enemy suit is flimsy.

(b) With only ♡Q–x it would be pure 'shooting' to bid in no-trumps at this stage. *Ask* your partner if he can help to boost your own partial heart stop by making a directional asking bid (DAB) of 3♡. North will give priority to a rebid of 3NT if he can help to stop the suit. If he can't, he will make the most sensible rebid available and you will know that your ♡Q–x isn't going to be enough to make 3NT a good contract.

(Bids: 2NT and 3♡)

26
♠ A J 8
♡ Q 6
◇ K Q J 8 3
♣ A 9 8

Game All, dealer South:

	S	W	N	E		S	W	N	E
(a)	1◇	1♠	2♣	No	(b)	1◇	No	1♡	2♣
	?					?			

Answers:

(a) With 17 points and a good stop in West's spades, again the best rebid is 2NT. It's true that you have only ♡Q–x, an unbid suit, but North has responded at the two-level without his own ace, and it's odds-on that he will have something in hearts.

(b) Here South has a guard in the clubs bid by East, but it is very possible that if a final contract of 3NT can be placed with declarer as North, it will be safer. If, for example, North holds ♣Q–x, a club lead from East would turn this into a double stop or, alternatively, the defence would have to give up a defensive tempo by attacking in another suit. So again, instead of just bidding 3NT, make a directional asking bid of 3♣ in the hope that North can bid 3NT.

(Bids: 2NT and 3♣)

27
♠ 8 6
♡ Q 9 7
◇ A 10 7 6 4
♣ Q 5 2

Love All, dealer North:

	N	E	S	W		N	E	S	W
(a)	1♣	No	1◇	1♡	(b)	1♣	No	1◇	1♠
	2♡	No	?			2♠	No	?	

Answers:

(a) North has made a directional asking bid enquiring whether South has a partial heart stop which will help to 'boost' his own heart holding, with a view to a final contract of 3NT. South can do this, so should give priority to a response in no-trumps. In this case he is only strong enough to bid 2NT, but note that, if he had a stronger hand, it would be up to him to bid 3NT, not a mere 2NT which would leave the onus on North.

(b) Again North has made a directional asking bid, though this time in spades, a suit in which South can do nothing to help. He must, therefore, make the most sensible rebid his hand suggests, in this case 3♣.

(Bids: 2NT and 3♣)

28
♠ 9
♡ 10
◇ Q J 8 5 4
♣ K J 5 4 3 2

Game to E–W, dealer West:

	W	N	E	S		W	N	E	S
(a)	1♡	No	1♠	?	(b)	1♠	No	3♠	?

Answers:

(a) Here we come to the use of the unusual no-trump, which simply means a bid in no-trumps in a situation where it really cannot show a genuine wish to play in that denomination. If South bids 1NT at this point, it would show a strong hand with stops in both majors. What he has in mind, however, is a possible sacrifice in clubs or diamonds, so he bids 2NT asking for North's preference between the *two unbid suits*. A further bid by West would let North off the hook of responding to this bid, though he may well be able to judge that a sacrifice contract of 5♣ or 5◇ would be worthwhile, even if doubled.

(b) In this sequence only one major suit has been bid by East–West and South, by bidding 3NT, could not possibly be showing a wish to play in that contract. He is asking, not for North's choice between the three unbid suits, but for his choice between the *minors*.

(Bids: 2NT and 3NT)

29
♠ K 10 9 2
♡ 8 3
◇ K J 7 6
♣ A Q 6

Game to N–S, dealer West:

	W	N	E	S		W	N	E	S
(a)	3♡	3♠	No	4♠	(b)	3♡	3♠	No	4♠
	No	4NT–		?		No	4NT	5♡	?

Answers:

(a) This is easy – the response to a Blackwood 4NT when you hold one ace is 5◊, so that's the correct bid here.

(b) Doubtless East passed on the first round seeing no need to interfere until he saw that North–South were trying for a slam. At this point he came to life and bid 5♡, preparing for a sacrifice, and also interfering with South's normal response to his partner's Blackwood 4NT. In these circumstances the responses are modified, a pass showing no ace, five of the next higher ranking suit one ace, and so on. So here South should bid 5♠.

(Bids: 5◊ and 5♠)

30   Game to N–S, dealer West:
♠ A K J 8 6 3   W   N   E   S   W   N   E   S
♡ A   (a) No   No   1♡   2♡   (b) No   No   1NT*?
◊ A Q 10 9 7 2   No   3♣   No   ?   *12–14 points
♣ –

Answers:

(a) The initial 2♡ cue-bid showed a powerful hand unsuitable for a take-out double, to which North has responded, not unexpectedly, with 3♣. The 2♡ bid is forcing to game. So North should show 4-card suits in *ascending* order until game has been reached.

(b) South doesn't want to defend on this hand which makes it impossible for him to double. The correct bid is the Acol conventional 2NT, showing a powerful two-suiter. This is forcing to game, and North must reply as he would to a take-out double. Thereafter South will have a chance to show both suits and North will steer the contract into the one which fits his hand best.

(Bids: 3♡ and 2NT)

Competition quiz

In competition against another player, one should answer the three questions in the **A** set, and the other the three questions in the **B** set on each page. In each case the dealer is the first-named player in the auction, and South's bid – or next bid – in the relative sequence is required. The score, unless otherwise stated, is Love All.

1A

1	♠ Q74				2	♠ KJ763				3	♠ K76
	♡ KJ963					♡ 852					♡ Q65
	◇ 1086					◇ A7					◇ A973
	♣ 64					♣ Q63					♣ A62

N	E	S	W		W	N	E	S		N	E	S	W
1♡	2♣	?			No	1◇	1♡	?		No	1◇	?	

Answers:

Bid		Reason
(2 points)		(3 points)
1	2♡	Provided a responding hand is suitable for a limit-bid, an intervening bid makes no difference at all.
2	1♠	Nothing about East's 1♡ intervention has interfered with your natural response of 1♠.
3	No Bid	As opener you would doubtless have bid 1NT (weak) but you have no playing strength. Pass and bid later if expedient.

1B

1	♠ A7				2	♠ 95				3	♠ A94
	♡ KJ653					♡ Q86					♡ 76
	◇ 974					◇ J107					◇ Q72
	♣ Q63					♣ KJ742					♣ KJ983

N	E	S	W		N	E	S	W		N	E	S	W
No	1♠	?			1♡	2◇	?			1♡	2♣	?	

Answers:

Bid		Reason
(2 points)		(3 points)
1	No Bid	This hand is very similar to 2 above, but this time you would be forced into bidding at the two-level – highly dangerous without better playing strength.
2	2♡	This hand is not strong enough to show the clubs at the three-level so, in spite of the lack of four-card heart support, it is wiser to give a simple raise in hearts.

3   Dbl   Just the sort of hand that makes it so dangerous to intervene at the two-level without adequate playing strength.

2A

1	♠ A 9 8	2	♠ 7 2	3	♠ K 10 5 4
	♡ J 9 6 4		♡ K J 10 8 5		♡ K J 9 6
	◇ A 6 3		◇ A Q 6		◇ A 7 4
	♣ Q 8 5		♣ 8 5 3		♣ 8 6

W	N	E	S		N	E	S	W		N	E	S	W
1♡	No	No	?		1♠	2♡	?			1♠	2♡	?	

Answers:

Bid		Reason
(2 points)		(3 points)

1   1NT   Comparing this with **1A**, 3 you might think you should pass, but this time you are in the protective position, where 1NT shows 11–15 points with a guard in the suit opened. Quite different values are needed for re-opening the bidding after two passes.

2   Dbl   With such poor support for North's spades, this is the most probable way of gaining a plus score on the deal.

3   3♠   Without the intervening 2♡ you would have raised to 3♠ and should do so now. Your spade support is too good to expect this suit to yield a comfortable number of tricks in defence.

2B

1	♠ K J 10 3	2	♠ A J 9 3	3	♠ 9 4
	♡ A 9 2		♡ K 10 8		♡ 8 6
	◇ Q J 6		◇ A J 6		◇ J 10 9
	♣ A J 7		♣ 9 6 5		♣ Q 10 9 8 5 3

E	S	W	N		W	N	E	S		W	N	E	S
1♠	?				1◇	No	No	?		1♡	1NT	No	?

Answers:

Bid		Reason
(2 points)		(3 points)

1   1NT   Used as an overcall, 1NT is *always strong*, irrespective of the agreed strength of the opening no-trump. It shows a minimum of 15, if not more, points with a double guard in the suit bid.

2   Dbl   In the protective position you should double on a hand of 9 or more points on which you would also be happy to defend if partner converts to a business double by passing. Note that the hand is not suitable for a protective 1NT or a cue-bid of 2♢.

3   2♣   South should treat North's 1NT overcall as he would a strong no-trump opening except that 2♣ is a natural weak take-out and not a fit-finding bid unless Stayman is used in this situation by agreement.

3A

1	♠ A J 9 3	2	♠ K 7 3	3	♠ K 7
	♡ K 10 8		♡ K Q 8 5 4		♡ A K J 7 6 5
	♢ A J 6		♢ Q 7		♢ 9 6 3
	♣ 9 6 5		♣ 9 6 2		♣ 8 4

E	S	W	N	W	N	E	S	W	N	E	S
1♠	?			1♢	No	No	?	No	No	1♠	?

Answers:

Bid		Reason
(2 points)		(3 points)

1   No Bid   This is the same hand as **2B**, 2 and in this position there is no sensible bid to make. Pass – your main hope is that West will also pass and North will be able to make a protective double, which you would pass happily.

2   1♡   You should generally re-open the bidding on as little as 9 points if you can do this at the one-level. Here South has 10 points and can bid 1♡ without fear of misleading North.

3   2♡   The ♠K is well-placed over the opening bid and the

excellent six-card suit in addition makes this hand well worth an attempt at competition.

3B

1	♠ A 6	2	♠ K 7 3	3	♠ K J 9 2
	♡ A K J 7 6 5		♡ K Q J 8 5 4		♡ A J 7 4
	◇ K 10 9		◇ 9 6		◇ 10
	♣ 9 2		♣ A 5		♣ A J 6 3

W	N	E	S	W	N	E	S	W	N	E	S
No	No	1♠	?	1◇	No	No	?	1◇	No	No	?

Answers:

Bid		Reason
(2 points)		(3 points)
1	3♡	You can't leave North to think you have nothing better than hand 3 at the top of this page. Jump one step, strong and invitational but not forcing.
2	2♡	This time you can't let North think you have only a modest little collection like 2 above. Jump one step to show the excellent suit plus outside values.
3	2◇	Not a hand for a protective double because you don't want to defend if North's pass were based on good diamonds. Cue-bid 2◇, forcing to suit agreement, which means that once a suit fit has been found the auction can be dropped below game level. Equally it is up to both North and South to bid on if a game seems likely.

4A

1	♠ A Q 9 5	2	♠ K Q J 8 5 4	3	♠ A J 7 4 2
	♡ K J 8 4		♡ A		♡ K J 9 5
	◇ 7 3		◇ 4		◇ K J 6
	♣ K J 9		♣ A K J 10 7		♣ 7

E	S	W	N	E	S	W	N	E	S	W	N
1◇	?			1◇	?			1NT*?			
								*12–14 points			

Answers:

Bid		Reason
(2 points)		(3 points)

1 Dbl Obviously South must try to compete on this hand, but it is one on which he would like to discuss with North, rather than tell him, their best final denomination.

2 2♢ South can't sensibly double to ask for North's choice of suit – North must be told at once that South's hand is not suitable for a double. A cue-bid of the suit opened is the correct choice.

3 2♢ Some form of defence to a no-trump opening is a 'must' for your armoury, and examples here are based on Astro. A bid of 2♢ shows nine cards between spades and one of the other suits.

4B

1 ♠ Q 9 2	2 ♠ 7 3	3 ♠ K Q 8 6
♡ K Q J 9 8 5	♡ K J 5	♡ A J 10 7
♢ A 6	♢ Q 10 8 2	♢ 10
♣ K 2	♣ A J 5 4	♣ A Q 9 3

E	S	W	N	N	E	S	W	W	N	E	S
1NT*?				1♠	Dbl	?		1♢	No	No	2♢
*12–14 points								No	2♠	No	?

Answers:

Bid	Reason
(2 points)	(3 points)

1 Dbl To bid 2♡ would be craven – this is an ideal hand for a business (*not* a take-out) double. It contains a good suit in which to attack and the best chance of a good plus score will come from defence.

2 Re-dbl This shows a minimum of 9 points, no particular fit for North's suit, and a probable interest in doubling the final contract reached by E–W. It also promises the ability to make a further bid.

3 4♠ As the 2♢ cue-bid is forcing to suit agreement only, it is up to South, if he thinks the combined hands will

produce a game, to bid it, and not to leave it to North.

5A

1	♠ K 9 7 3			2	♠ A 9 3			3	♠ 9 6 3		
	♡ J 8				♡ Q 10 7				♡ Q J 7 5 4 2		
	◇ J 6 2				◇ J 6 4				◇ 8		
	♣ 10 8 5 4				♣ 10 8 5 4				♣ 8 5 4		

N	E	S	W	N	E	S	W	N	E	S	W
1♠	Dbl	?		1◇	Dbl	?		1◇	Dbl		?

Answers:

Bid		Reason
(2 points)		(3 points)

1 2♠ Without the intervening double you would only just scrape up a single raise. After the double you may make such a bid on even less than normal values, for its pre-emptive effect.

2 1NT After an intervening double 1NT is used as a pre-emptive nuisance-bid, showing 7–8 points, or just possibly a 'bad' 9 points, (cf. **4B**, 2) which are not worth a redouble.

3 1♡ After the double a simple change-of-suit is no longer a one round force. It is a rescue bid warning partner of a poor fit for his suit and a playable suit of your own.

5B

1	♠ Q J 7 5 4 2			2	♠ 9 3			3	♠ K J 9 2		
	♡ 9 6 3				♡ K Q J 7 5 4				♡ K 10 6 4		
	◇ 8				◇ A 6 3				◇ A 9 2		
	♣ 8 5 4				♣ J 10				♣ 6 4		

N	E	S	W	N	E	S	W	N	E	S	W
1♡	Dbl	?		1◇	Dbl	?		1♠	Dbl		?

Answers:

Bid		Reason
(2 points)		(3 points)

1 No Your clue comes from 3 above. Had North been
   Bid doubled in 1◇ you would have rescued into 1♠. As it

is, with a three-card fit, don't rescue into something which may not be so good.

2   2♡   Again your clue is in 3 above, as you must distinguish between a weak 'rescue operation' and a genuine bid with a good playable suit. 2♡ is a one-round force after the double, not a game force as it would be otherwise.

3   2NT   Following a double both the single and double raise limit-bids are used pre-emptively on reduced values. A genuine full-strength limit raise to the three-level is shown by a *conventional* response of 2NT.

6A

1	♠ K Q 10 8 6 4	2	♠ K 8 6 5	3	♠ K J 9
	♡ J 9		♡ A J 9 2		♡ Q 9 7 4
	◊ 7 2		◊ 6		◊ A 6 3
	♣ A 8 5		♣ Q 10 8 4		♣ A J 7

S	W	N	E	N	E	S	W	S	W	N	E
1♠	Dbl	Re-dbl	No	1◊	Dbl	Re-dbl	No	1♣	Dbl	1♠	No
?				No	1♡	?		?			

Answers:

Bid	Reason
(2 points)	(3 points)

1   2♠   By his redouble, North showed willingness to defend East–West's contract, probably doubling at his next turn. Tell him this is highly unattractive on your light opener by taking out.

2   Dbl   Your redouble showed at least 9 points and a probable wish to double the final East–West contract. What could be more what the doctor ordered? North has shown willingness to co-operate by his pass.

3   No Bid   You opened 1♣ being too strong for 1NT. Remember the sort of hand North is showing (cf. **5A**, 3) and pass.

6B

1	♠ K 7 9	2	♠ K Q 7 4 3	3	♠ K Q 10 8 6 4
	♡ Q 9 7 4		♡ A J 9		♡ J 9
	◇ A 6 3		◇ K Q 6		◇ 7 2
	♣ A J 7		♣ Q 6		♣ A 8 5

S	W	N	E	S	W	N	E	S	W	N	E
1♣	Dbl	2NT	No	1♠	Dbl	Re-	No	1♠	Dbl	2NT	No
						dbl					
?				?				?			

Answers:

Bid	Reason
(2 points)	(3 points)

1   3NT   Compare 3 above and **5B**, 3. If North raised 1♣ to 3♣ without the intervening double you'd try 3NT, and it's only common sense to try it now.

2   No   Give North the chance he has asked for, which is to
    Bid   bid again. West has yet to make his self-rescue attempt, and you will be glad to defend anything North may double. If West should pass you could be in many a worse contract than this!

3   3♠   Without the double, had North raised your 1♠ to 3♠, you would have passed. So now convert his conventional 2NT to 3♠.

7A

1	♠ K Q 7 5 3	2	♠ J 8 6 5 3	3	♠ Q 10 9 4
	♡ A J 6		♡ 9 2		♡ Q J 6 2
	◇ A J 5 4		◇ 8 7 4		◇ K 8 4
	♣ 7		♣ 9 8 7		♣ 7 6

S	W	N	E	W	N	E	S	W	N	E	S
1♠	Dbl	Re-	2◇	1◇	Dbl	1♡	?	1♡	Dbl	No	?
		dbl									
?											

Answers:

Bid	Reason
(2 points)	(3 points)

1   Dbl   North, by his original redouble, has shown a probable

desire to defend East–West's final contract (doubled).
Tell him that you can go along with this, and can
yourself cope with the diamond suit.

2   1♠   North, by his double, has *asked* you which suit you
prefer. Help him out, never forgetting, of course, the
type of hand East should have.

3   1NT If, as I hope, you have adopted the Herbert negative,
you don't want to bid 1♠ here. You can, however,
perfectly well bid 1NT, showing a better-than-bust
and stop in hearts.

7B

1	♠ J 7		2	♠ K J 7		3	♠ J 10
	♡ 8 6 5 3			♡ K J 9			♡ Q 10 8 5
	◇ 9 4 2			◇ A J 6			◇ K 7 5 4 2
	♣ 10 9 7 5			♣ A 7 5 4			♣ 8 4

W	N	E	S		S	W	N	E		W	N	E	S
1♡	Dbl	No	?		1♣	Dbl	1♡	1♠		1♣	Dbl	No	?
					?								

Answers:

Bid	Reason
(2 points)	(3 points)

1   1♠   This is a true 'bust'. Bid a Herbert 1♠ to warn North.
2   2♡   Remembering the type of hand North will have, 2♡ is
quite enough at this stage, *not* the 2NT you would bid
in an uninterrupted sequence.
3   1♡   Apart from the fact that you should always show a
major suit if you can, 1◇ would be the Herbert
negative, a bid you can avoid.

8A

1	♠ A 9 7 2		2	♠ K J 10 7 5 3		3	♠ Q 6
	♡ K J 10 5			♡ 9 5			♡ 8 2
	◇ 6			◇ K 6			◇ Q J 10 9 6 3
	♣ K 9 8 4			♣ J 7 4			♣ J 10 8

W	N	E	S		W	N	E	S		W	N	E	S
1◇	Dbl	No	?		1♡	Dbl	No	?		1◇	Dbl	No	?

Answers:

Bid		Reason
(2 points)		(3 points)
1	2◇	Cue-bid 2◇, the suit opened – and doubled – which passes the buck back to North to make the choice.
2	2♠	Apart from the fact that 1♠ would be negative, it is essential to distinguish, for North's sake, between a suit of this value and one such as you held in **7B**, 3.
3	No Bid	Convert North's take-out double to a business one by passing, surely your best chance of a good plus score on the hand.

8B

1	♠ K Q 9 7	2	♠ 9 5	3	♠ A J 9 4
	♡ K 8 5		♡ K J 10 7 5 3		♡ K J 8 3
	◇ A K 6		◇ K 6		◇ 6
	♣ K J 3		♣ J 7 4		♣ K 10 7 4

W	N	E	S	W	N	E	S	W	N	E	S
1◇	No	No	?	1♠	Dbl	No	?	1◇	Dbl	No	2◇
								No	2♡	No	?

Answers:

Bid		Reason
(2 points)		(3 points)
1	2NT	This shows 19–20 balanced points. North will almost certainly take out into a suit, after which you can decide whether to go for a game in his suit or in no-trumps.
2	2♡	Comparing this with 2 above you might want to bid 3♡, but this will cramp the auction. Partner will not miss the fact that you did not bid a negative 2◇.
3	4♡	As your 2◇ was forcing to suit agreement only, you could pass. On the other hand, your values facing North who could double must surely be worth a try for game.

9A

1	♠ K 10 8 5	2	♠ A K 10 7 4	3	♠ A 10 9 2
	♡ Q 10 9		♡ A J 8		♡ K 9 8 4
	◇ K 8 2		◇ Q 6		◇ K J 6
	♣ 9 7 3		♣ K J 5		♣ J 3

N	E	S	W	S	W	N	E	N	E	S	W
1♠	2◇	2♠	No	1♠	2◇	2♡	No	1♣	1◇	1♠	No
3♣	No	?		?				2◇	No	?	

Answers:

Bid	Reason
(2 points)	(3 points)

1   3♠   3♣ in this situation is a trial bid, just as it would be without East's 2◇ intervention. However, there's nothing to be done by South except sign-off in 3♠.

2   3◇   This is a directional asking bid designed to discover whether 3NT, 4♡, or 4♠ will be the best final contract. If North can help with a partial stop in diamonds he will give priority to a rebid in no-trumps.

3   3NT   This time it is North who is making a directional asking bid. With a very adequate diamond stop and 12½ points, South should give an affirmative reply of 3NT, not a mere 2NT.

9B

1	♠ A K 9 7 3	2	♠ 9	3	♠ A J 6
	♡ K J 7		♡ K J 9 8 5		♡ Q 4
	◇ K J 6		◇ Q 10 7 6		◇ A Q J 6 3
	♣ Q 4		♣ A J 7		♣ A 10 7

S	W	N	E	W	N	E	S	S	W	N	E
1♠	No	2◇	2♡	1♠	2♣	2♠	?	1◇	No	1♡	2♣
?								?			

Answers:

Bid	Reason
(2 points)	(3 points)

1   2NT   This shows the count and heart guard. It's true South has only ♣Q–x, but North has bid at the two-level without his own ◇K–J and he must have something!

2   3♣   Responding to an intervening bid is different from responding to an opening bid. South's simple change-of-suit would not be forcing, so support for what must be at least a five-card suit should be shown in preference to a new suit of doubtful value.

3   3♣   Another DAB. If North has as much as ♣Q–x, 3NT is likely to play better from his hand than from South's. There's plenty of time to decide on the best final contract.

10A

1	♠ K J 7	2	♠ 7 3	3	♠ K 10 9 3
	♡ A 9 6 2		♡ Q 9 2		♡ Q 8 7 4
	◇ 8		◇ A 10 8 6 5		◇ Q 6
	♣ A 10 7 5 2		♣ Q 8 3		♣ 8 4 2

E	S	W	N	N	E	S	W	N	E	S	W
1NT*?				1♣	1♡	2◇	No	No	1NT*	No	No
*12–14 points				2♡	No	?		2♣	No	?	
								*12–14 points			

Answers:

Bid	Reason
(2 points)	(3 points)

1   2♣   This bid, in the Astro defence, takes the place of a double (which would be for business) when you want to compete against a no-trump opening but are not strong enough to double. Note that 2♣ shows 9 cards between hearts and one of the minors.

2   2NT   North's 2♡ is a directional asking bid. South must confirm that he holds at least a partial guard in hearts.

3   No   When a player has previously passed (using Astro) his
    Bid   2♣ or 2◇ becomes natural and not a conventional take-out request.

10B

1	♠ 6	2	♠ A 7	3	♠ A J 8 6 3
	♡ K 4		♡ K Q 10 9 6 5		♡ K J 9 2
	◊ K J 9 7 2		◊ 8 3		◊ A 7
	♣ A 10 9 7 3		♣ Q 6 2		♣ 3 2

E	S	W	N	W	N	E	S	W	N	E	S
1NT*	2◊	No	2♡	1NT*	2♣	No	?	1NT	2◊	No	?
No	?										

*12–14 points   *12–14 points   *12–14 points

Answers:

Bid		Reason
(2 points)		(3 points)
1	3♣	North will have understood 2◊ as a take-out request with a void or singleton club. Now 3♣ shows a minor two-suiter.
2	3♡	In response to North's Astro 2♣ this hand is too good for a mere 2♡. 3♡ shows a good playable suit and is highly invitational, not forcing.
3	2NT	This conventionally passes the buck back to North to pick his own best suit. It is forcing to the four-level only, that is, to a major-suit game if a fit is found.

11A

1	♠ K 3	2	♠ –	3	♠ 7 4
	♡ –		♡ 5		♡ 6 2
	◊ K J 7 3 2		◊ 10 8 7 6 5 3		◊ K J 6
	♣ Q 10 9 6 3 2		♣ J 9 6 5 3 2		♣ A Q J 7 5 3

Game to E–W:				Game to E–W:				Game All:			
W	N	E	S	N	E	S	W	W	N	E	S
1♠	No	3♡	?	No	1♠	No	3♡	1♠	2◊	2♡	?
				No	4♡	?					

Answers:

Bid		Reason
(2 points)		(3 points)
1	3NT	With an apparently worthless hand in defence of what is going to be at least a vulnerable game contract,

South suggests a sacrifice in one of the two unbid suits, by a bid in no-trumps when this cannot possibly show a genuine wish to play in that denomination.

2   4NT South passed initially to see whether East–West were going to reach a game contract. Now not only a game, but a slam contract seems probable and a sacrifice in one or other of the two unbid suits must surely be profitable.

3   3◇   With adequate diamond support, raise North's suit rather than show even a six-card club suit (cf. **9B**, 2 on p. 226).

11B

1	♠ A K J 8 6 4	2	♠ 7 6	3	♠ Q 10 5
	♡ –		♡ K J 9		♡ K 9 7 3
	◇ A K J 6 5		◇ A Q 9 8 2		◇ 8
	♣ K 5		♣ Q 7 5		♣ K Q 7 5 2

E	S	W	N	N	E	S	W	W	N	E	S
1NT*	?			1♣	1♡	2◇	No	No	1♠	2NT	?
				2♡	No	?					

*12–14 points

Answers:

Bid	Reason
(2 points)	(3 points)

1   2NT Far too good for a simple take-out request and unsuitable for a double. Use the Acol conventional bid of 2NT, a game force showing a powerful two-suiter, and asking North to show his best suit as he would if responding to a take-out double.

2   3NT Compare **10A**, 2, where you only answered a DAB with 2NT. Never leave to partner what you are good enough to do yourself, so here bid 3NT.

3   No   East has used an unusual no-trump bid asking West
     Bid   for his choice between the *minors*. You have been warned off bidding clubs, so pass and await developments.

12A

1	♠ K 10 8 6	2	♠ K Q J 8 5 4	3	♠ A K Q 10 7 4
	♡ 6 5 3		♡ A		♡ 8 5
	◇ Q 7		◇ 4		◇ A Q
	♣ Q 10 8 3		♣ A K J 10 7		♣ K Q J

W	N	E	S	E	S	W	N	E	S	W	N
1♠	2NT	3♣	?	1◇	2◇	No	2♡	1◇	2◇	No	2♡
				No	?			No	?		

Answers:

Bid		Reason
(2 points)		(3 points)
1	4♣	North's bid is the unusual no-trump requesting your choice between the minor suits with a possible sacrifice contract in mind. Your preference for clubs is too strong for you to take the opportunity, provided by East's bid, to pass. If North wants to bid on, you can go along with him.
2	3♠	This will show North that your interest is in the black suits, not hearts.
3	2♠	Even if North has a complete bust you want him to keep open until a game contract is reached. He knows, however, that you were too strong for a jump bid of 2♠ on the first round and will show four-card suits in ascending order and you will repeat spades.

12B

1	♠ K J 10 9 7	2	♠ 8 5	3	♠ 9 3 2
	♡ A Q J 10 4		♡ A K Q 10 7 4		♡ 9 8 6 4
	◇ –		◇ K Q J		◇ 8 7 6
	♣ K Q 6		♣ A Q		♣ 5 4 3

E	S	W	N	E	S	W	N	E	S	W	N
1◇	2◇	No	2♠	1♣	2♣	No	2◇	1♠	No	2◇	2NT
No	?			No	2♡	No	2♠	No	?		
				No	?						

Answers:

| Bid | Reason |
| (2 points) | (3 points) |

1   4♠   Eureka! North has a four-card spade suit! Even if it's only 8-high there is a good chance for game, so bid it.

2   3♡   Reading you for possibly a spade-heart two-suiter, North is showing preference for spades. Confirm your single-suited hand by a heart rebid. North will surely put you to 4♡.

3   3♡   North has shown a desire to compete in one of the unbid suits, hearts or clubs. You have no option but to tell him which you prefer as East has not let you off the hook by rebidding.

Index